# *The Cognitive Framework Model*

*How the Building Blocks of Our Identity Form Our Subjective Reality*

# Charles R.W. Sears

# Acknowledgment

O ur collective knowledge builds upon the contributions of those who came before us—from ancient civilizations that developed language to the personal relationships that shape our understanding. This exploration into human psychology has been made possible by numerous individuals who have supported, challenged, and refined these ideas.

Gratitude begins with my parents, who created an environment that encouraged curiosity and the pursuit of deeper understanding. My teachers, particularly Mr. Eric Hansen, provided influential leadership that continues to shape my approach to examining self-perception and identity formation. My business partner, Xavier Canez, for becoming a student of this ideology and, by learning, helped me fully articulate the thoughts that became this book.

Special thanks to Dr. Daniel Davis, whose academic expertise in sociology proved invaluable. His rigorous review ensured accuracy in cited research and theories, while his contributions to the book's illustrations enhance reader understanding of complex concepts. His guidance was instrumental in shaping and refining this work.

To each of these contributors, my sincere appreciation.

T o my wife, who endured countless late-night discussions about correlations and conclusions, listened patiently as I worked through half-formed ideas, and challenged my thinking so thoroughly that she can now explain my own framework better than I can. This book exists because of your unwavering support, your sharp intellect, and your willingness to be both my greatest encourager and most honest critic.

# Table of contents

ONE

---

# *Overview of the Cognitive Framework Model*

E very human being constructs an internal narrative about who they are—a mental framework that determines how they interpret experiences, make decisions, and navigate relationships. This framework, which we call identity, operates largely beneath conscious awareness yet drives nearly every aspect of human behavior.

Traditional approaches to understanding identity have been fragmented. Sociologists examine cultural influences, psychologists focus on cognitive processes, neuroscientists study brain mechanisms, and philosophers explore consciousness. Each discipline offers valuable insights, but none provides a complete picture of how identity actually forms and functions.

This fragmentation creates practical problems. Mental health professionals lack comprehensive frameworks for identity-related issues. Individuals seeking self-improvement miss crucial connections between different psychological processes.

This book presents an integrated model that bridges these gaps. Drawing from psychology, philosophy, neuroscience, and real-world application, we'll explore how identity forms through the interaction of cognitive processes, social influences, and personal experiences. More importantly, we'll examine how understanding this system leads to practical improvements in mental health and personal development.

You'll discover how "fast" and "slow" thinking shape your sense of self, why early experiences create lasting patterns, and how social contexts influence identity development. We'll explore the strengths and vulnerabilities of the human identity system, providing concrete tools for optimization and repair.

Whether you're a mental health professional, researcher, or someone seeking deeper self-understanding, this framework offers practical insights you can apply immediately.

Let's begin by examining what identity actually is and how it forms.

## Building Blocks of the Framework

When attempting to comprehend the workings of the mind, there are generally two main approaches: biological and cognitive. The first investigates the physical structure of the brain and the interactions among its components–it investigates the hardware. The second focuses on the mental processes of the brain and the outcomes they generate–it focuses on the software.

When studying the functioning and processes of the mind, students often encounter concepts that stem from both top-down (cognitive, or the "software") and bottom-up (biological, or the "hardware") approaches. The cognitive approach involves analyzing higher-level mental functions and their influence on lower-level processes, while the biological approach examines how simple neural interactions give rise to complex cognitive functions.

These concepts often address how we manage important aspects of life, such as regulating emotions, coping with trauma, or overcoming addiction. In this chapter, we will zoom out on both of these systems to understand them as a whole—taking a philosophical approach to understanding how the mind forms the scaffolding or, "what it believes to be true about the world around it." Later we explore how the mind uses this scaffolding to predict future outcomes and respond accordingly.

## Basic Terminology

Let's begin with a few basic terms that will be used regularly with this model: beginning at the foundational layer with observations, then moving up to correlations, conclusions, and values (See figure 1).

## Observations and Correlations

At the most basic level, we observe a multitude of things all around us. Through our senses, we absorb a constant stream of data. Imagine walking through a bustling city street: the vibrant colors of storefronts, the cacophony of honking horns, the scent of freshly brewed coffee wafting from a café. Each of these sensory inputs forms an observation, a snapshot of the world around us.

But our experiences don't end there. Our minds possess an incredible capacity to store these observations as memories. Picture this: you're sitting on a beach, feeling the warm sand beneath your toes, and listening to the soothing sound of crashing waves. Later, when you close your eyes and think back to that moment, you can recall the texture of the sand, the rhythm of the waves, and even the taste of salty sea air. These memories serve as a repository, preserving our observations and allowing us to revisit them in our minds.

Our minds, however, go far beyond merely storing individual observations. As we take in this information, our mind is hard at work under the hood seeking to identify connections and patterns. At the biological level this has to do with electric signaling across neurons and synapses[3], but at the cognitive level, a less visible process is underway.

Imagine encountering a series of unfortunate events: a flat tire during your morning commute, a spilled cup of coffee that ruins your favorite shirt, and a missed deadline at work. While these incidents may appear disconnected, your mind strives to find patterns and connections to prevent their recurrence. It might interpret these events as "bad luck" or a prolonged streak of misfortune. Yet, with focused introspection, you may start recognizing a common thread— the habit of hitting the snooze button on your alarm clock. You hit the snooze button every morning hoping for a few more minutes of rest. This additional time in bed leads to less time to prepare for the day, causing you to run late to work. As you speed through traffic, you have to hit your brakes often, increasing your chances of spilling your coffee on your shirt. Your hurried state led to a lack of attention, causing you to miss the pile of broken glass in your street lane. You hit it, causing your flat tire. This takes time to fix, making you miss your deadline at work. Through careful reflection, your mind begins forming correlations and associations, constructing a framework that helps make sense of the world around you.

The process of drawing correlations between observations can be both conscious and subconscious. For example, you might notice a recurring pattern of rainy days every time you plan an outdoor activity. This observation could lead you to associate rain with canceled plans, prompting you to prepare alternative arrangements in the future. Similarly, you may notice a connection between stressful situations and the onset of a particular physical symptom, such as a headache. By recognizing this correlation, you become more aware of the impact of stress on your well-being and can take proactive steps to manage it.

In essence, our ability to *observe* and store information forms the bedrock of our mental framework. By recognizing the richness of our sensory experiences and the associations or *correlations* we draw between them, we gain valuable insights into our own minds and the world around us.

## Conclusions

Correlations between our observations begin to cluster together through pattern recognition (a survival mechanism), eventually forming larger groupings known as "conclusions". These conclusions encompass the ideas and attitudes we have developed through countless encounters with the world. The strength of a conclusion increases as more correlations align with it. Some conclusions trace back to our earliest memories, while others are built upon them, further reinforcing our confidence in their validity and making them resistant to change. Throughout this text, I may occasionally use the term "beliefs" interchangeably with "conclusions" for stylistic purposes. However, I predominantly employ the term "conclusions" to denote an individual's subjective understanding of something. Let's consider the following sentences:

*"Her ideas challenged my conclusions."*

*"Her ideas challenged my beliefs."*

In the first sentence, you might feel inclined to fact-check the origins of your conclusions. In the second sentence, you might sense a defensive reaction. It is beneficial to approach our Framework with objectivity, at least until we comprehend the origins of our conclusions and determine whether we choose to uphold them.

## Values

Stepping back, these correlations amalgamate into conclusions, which in turn aggregate into more significant connections known as "values". Values are what we typically express to others and often occupy a more prominent place (top of mind awareness) in our consciousness than the multitude of underlying conclusions. While we may be able to articulate our values, understanding their origin and delving into the underlying mechanisms that shape them can often elude us.

Our personal frameworks encompass our entire comprehension of the world, shaping our assumptions, perceptions, and decision-making processes. They serve as the lens through which we perceive ourselves and the surrounding world. Our frameworks constitute a comprehensive network of connections within our minds, distinct from our memories but intricately linked to them through correlations.

It is important to note that when referring to the Framework Model or Framework Theory, I am not alluding to an individual person's internal framework. Instead, I present an educational structure that facilitates the understanding of how various leading brain and mind theories converge.

In other words, the Framework Model (see Figure 2) serves as an outline to grasp the operational dynamics of individual people's frameworks. To understand what observations, correlations, conclusions and values exist within an individual's framework, one would have to undertake an exploratory process requiring the subject be both in a state of "consideration", and responsive to structured questioning which we will cover in later chapters.

**Figure 1.** Layers of the Framework

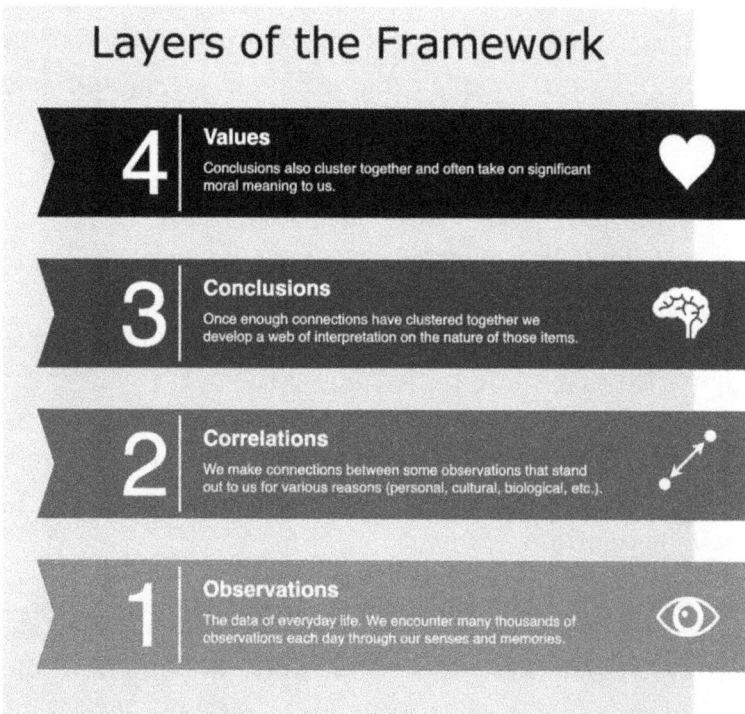

*This model illustrates how raw observations progress into correlations, conclusions, and ultimately values, showing the hierarchical structure through which meaning and significance are constructed.*

Our framework helps us perceive and make sense of the world around us. It is a cognitive structure that organizes and stores connections between data in our mind, enabling us to interpret new information from our environment quickly and effectively. Each individual's framework is unique and is shaped by our personal histories, cultural backgrounds, and social contexts. It is also constantly being modified and updated as we encounter new information and experiences.

Our frameworks fundamentally shape our values and how we interpret and respond to events, make decisions, and interact with others. As a dynamic and evolving mental model, it is not fixed or immutable, but is constantly influenced by our experiences and interactions with the world. Even though most of the framework exists at a subconscious level, it exists as part of the core of our identity.

**Figure 2. The Framework Model**

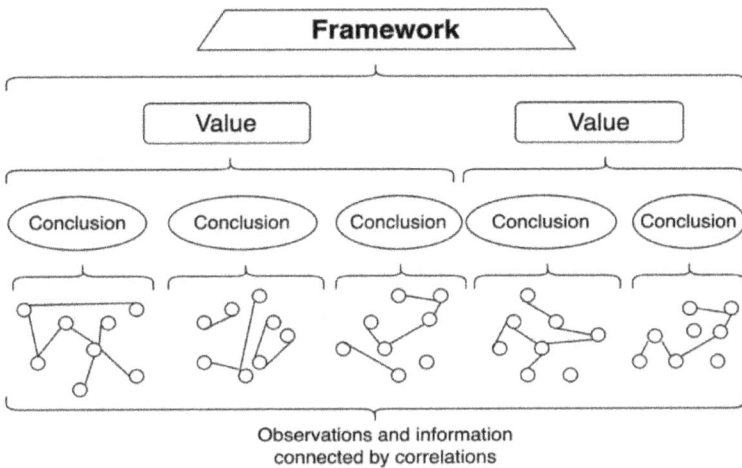

Observations and information
connected by correlations

*This diagram illustrates how observations, linked through correlations, form clusters of conclusions that accumulate into values. These values, in turn, integrate within a broader framework that organizes meaning and guides interpretation.*

See Figure 3 as an illustration of how complex this process can be, even around simple things like understanding what an apple is.

## **Figure 3.** Example Reasoning Pathway

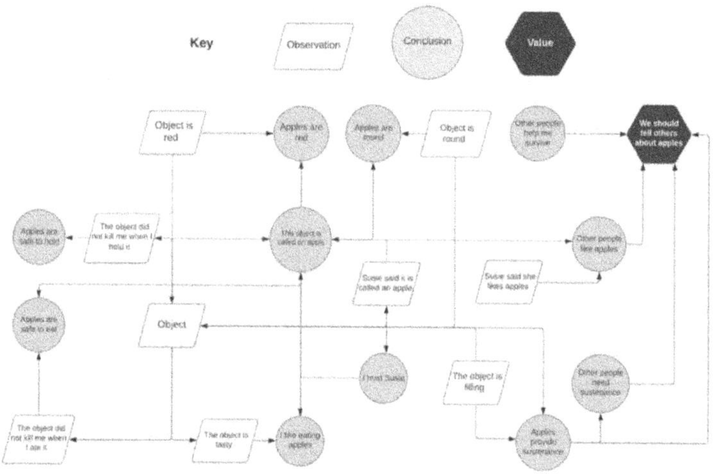

*This figure illustrates the complexity of how values—rules we live by—emerge from the simplest observations. Step by step, raw sensory data and experiences connect into correlations, build into conclusions, and ultimately cluster into values that guide behavior, showing how meaning and moral significance grow from ordinary encounters.*

By understanding this process, we can gain insight into how our thoughts and beliefs are shaped by the continuous intake and interpretation of data from our environment and experiences. This knowledge can help us become more self-aware because we may be able to recognize where the correlations building up our conclusions and values came from. We can become more empathetic toward others as well because we may be able to understand how the same processes happened for them.

For example, take the image above in Figure 3. The conclusions drawn about the apple are dependent on observations and other, previously drawn conclusions. For example, identification of the apple as "red" requires a previous understanding of what "red" visually looks like, as well as learning the term itself in the English language.

Additionally, part of the conclusion that this is an "apple" relies on commentary from a trusted source, "Susie." That conclusion wasn't formed from the basis of other known information about the apple, it was formed through a psychological process called "priming" and was accepted through the process of confirmation bias based on previously drawn conclusions about "Susie." For example, other conclusions such as "Susie's judgment is trustworthy" and "Susie's intentions are pure," which were formed from prior experiences, influence our decision to adopt this observation as our own conclusion.

What would happen if we removed that observation from this individual's framework? How would that impact other dependent conclusions? How would the shift in those conclusions impact the resulting value? This is a simple example of how we might conclude that an apple is an apple, and as well as what we "should" do with it. But you can take it further and consider any of the other areas in your framework that are also dependent on relationships from previous knowledge. What is the map of connections that lead up to your views on marriage, democracy, private property, or the value of higher education for example.

With this knowledge we are better equipped to adapt and grow in response to new information and experiences. The conclusions and values we have already formed may have happened with or without our intentional agency, but moving forward we can play a role in the outcome of this process.

Our frameworks are always active in our thinking and decision-making processes, particularly when we encounter new information or experiences. It serves as a cognitive structure that helps us organize and interpret this information and update our values accordingly. It can also influence our decision-making processes by guiding which information we attend to and how we weigh different pieces of information.

## The Framework in our Day-to-Day Lives: Fast and Slow Thinking

Here we will explore the relationship between the Framework Model and Daniel Kahneman's "System 1 and System 2 Thinking[4]," to illustrate how our frameworks influence our intuitive, automatic decision-making process. This will demonstrate our framework in action and underscore the importance of understanding its impact on our thinking. Furthermore, we will examine strategies for improving our framework by acknowledging cognitive biases, seeking alternative perspectives, and fostering self-awareness.

## System 1 Thinking: Fast and Reactive

Daniel Kahneman, a renowned psychologist and Nobel laureate, introduced the concept of "System 1 and System 2 Thinking" as a way to explain the dual nature of human decision-making processes. In his groundbreaking work, "Thinking, Fast and Slow," Kahneman presents two cognitive systems that work in tandem to shape our thoughts, judgments, and actions.

System 1 Thinking represents the fast, intuitive, automatic, and emotional component of our cognitive processes. This system operates effortlessly, using heuristics or mental shortcuts to quickly arrive at judgments and decisions. In many cases, System 1 Thinking is highly efficient, allowing us to react rapidly to stimuli and navigate our daily lives with ease. However, this mode of thinking is also prone to cognitive biases and errors. It relies on our existing mental models, or framework, informed by the emotional state we are in or "State of Mind" at the moment.

Our framework plays a significant role in shaping our System 1 Thinking as it serves as a structured mental repository for our beliefs or conclusions and our values. When we encounter new information or situations, we rapidly access our framework to make sense of the stimuli, drawing upon existing correlations and conclusions to inform our reactions.

In essence, our frameworks act as a cognitive filter influencing our intuitive responses based on our pre-existing beliefs and assumptions. Our framework shapes our perception of a situation, which can vary from person to person and circumstance to circumstance.

Recognizing the role of our framework in our System 1 Thinking is crucial. It can help us become more aware of the factors that shape our automatic responses and decision-making processes. By understanding the impact of our framework on our intuitive judgments, we can better identify potential cognitive biases and errors, and strive to improve the accuracy and effectiveness of our decision-making. This awareness can empower us to take a more mindful approach to our thoughts and actions, ultimately fostering personal growth and development.

To better understand the impact of our frameworks on our System 1 Thinking, let us consider a practical example. Imagine that you're walking down a busy street when you suddenly encounter a large, barking dog. Without conscious effort, your System 1 Thinking kicks in, rapidly drawing upon the existing correlations and conclusions stored in your framework to make sense of the situation and determine your response.

Suppose your framework includes positive correlations and conclusions about dogs based on pleasant experiences with friendly pets throughout your life. In this case, your System 1 Thinking may lead you to perceive the barking dog as non-threatening and approachable, resulting in a calm and unafraid response to it.

Conversely, if your framework includes negative correlations and conclusions about dogs, stemming from a previous encounter with an aggressive dog or hearing about a friend's frightening experience, your System 1 Thinking might trigger fear and prompt you to avoid the barking dog altogether.

Additionally, your cultural background, social context, and personal history play a significant role in shaping your framework and, consequently, your reactions to the barking dog. For instance, certain cultural beliefs might associate specific dog breeds with danger, leading you to perceive the dog as a threat even if you have no personal experiences to support this conclusion.

Perhaps you read Stephen King's 1981 novel "Cujo"[5] as a kid and have negative associations with St. Bernards. Similarly, in a social context, such as growing up in a neighborhood where certain dogs are commonly used as guard animals, this might also contribute to the development of a cautious or fearful response.

By examining the influence of our framework on our System 1 Thinking in real-life scenarios, we can better appreciate the complex interplay between our existing correlations, conclusions, and values, as well as our automatic decision-making processes. Recognizing the impact of our framework on our everyday thoughts and actions is essential for fostering self-awareness, understanding the origins of our cognitive biases, and striving for more balanced and accurate decision-making. Through this awareness, we can actively work to refine and improve our framework, ultimately leading to more informed and effective judgments in the complex world around us.

## System 2 Thinking: Slow and Reflective (Or Consideration)

System 2 Thinking, as described by Daniel Kahneman, involves slow, deliberate, and analytical thought processes. It is the mode of thinking that we engage in when we are faced with complex problems or situations that require conscious attention and effort.

System 2 Thinking allows us to examine information more thoroughly, evaluate evidence, and consider alternative perspectives before reaching a decision. In Framework Theory, I refer to this process as *consideration*. It happens by questioning the truth and accuracy of new information or existing elements of our framework. I will take up the process of consideration extensively in section three on ways to intentionally repair our frameworks.

While System 1 Thinking relies heavily on the existing correlations, conclusions, and values stored in our framework to make quick automatic decisions, System 2 Thinking, or consideration, allows us to scrutinize and challenge the assumptions and beliefs that underpin our framework.

For example, after the immediate fearful response to a St. Bernard dog mentioned previously, perhaps you wondered why you responded that way? You may have seen the comedy movie Beethoven[6] and remembered that this breed is usually quite friendly when they do not have rabies (as was the case in

Cujo). You calm down, and maybe even pet the dog. With your mind in a state of consideration, as you pet the dog and he proves to be friendly, you allow your correlations to be altered, reframing your conclusion that "St. Bernards are vicious and scary" to "St. Bernards can be nice and approachable". By Engaging in System 2 Thinking, we can consciously analyze the accuracy and validity of our framework's components and identify areas where it may be incomplete, biased, or outdated.

System 1 Thinking has its usefulness, because sometimes split-second decisions and actions do need to be made, especially to avoid danger. But overreliance on it in all situations can lead to problems.

By effectively employing System 2 Thinking in refining our framework, we can move closer to objective reality. To more effectively pursue our goal of understanding the world as it is and improving our chances of survival, we can adopt the following strategies centered around the questions "Is what I believe true?" and "Is the information I have true?" We enter into the process of consideration when we:

1. **Challenge assumptions:** An assumption is a thing we accept as true without proof. It may be based on observations but is often something we hold as a taken-for-granted expectation. However, each of our assumptions came from somewhere in our experience or history. These assumptions can be true or false. Therefore, we do well when we examine the conclusions that make up our framework by questioning their basis in objective truth. Ask yourself if your conclusions are

grounded in solid evidence or simply influenced by personal biases and preconceptions.

2. **Embrace alternative perspectives:** Actively seek out, conduct research, and consider new information that challenges your existing conclusions. This will help identify and address any gaps, inconsistencies, or falsehoods in your framework and align it more closely with objective reality. Everyone has a framework, and while two people from a similar culture may have significant overlap in their perspective on the world, no two frameworks are identical. Listening to the perceptions and conclusions of others can help us identify areas in our own framework that may need greater reflection.

3. **Engage in critical thinking:** Develop your critical thinking skills to better evaluate the quality and reliability of information and evidence, allowing you to make more informed decisions and refine your framework with objective truths. As much as we can learn from others, there is still greater value in seeking out information that is vetted with higher levels of legitimacy. Opinions can be written very persuasively, but what is the evidence behind an opinion that might move it into the realm of fact?

Ways of doing this are developed later in the book. For now, just know that by incorporating the process of consideration into our cognitive processes, we can consciously and deliberately analyze our framework, identify its limitations, and work towards refining it with objective truths. In doing so, we enhance our ability to make well-informed decisions that are grounded in a more accurate and comprehensive understanding of the world around us.

# References

[1] https://www.merriam-webster.com/dictionary/framework

[2]https://dictionary.cambridge.org/us/dictionary/english/framework

[3] https://mind.ilstu.edu/curriculum/neurons_intro/neurons_intro.html

[4] Kahneman, D. (2011). Thinking, Fast and Slow. United Kingdom: Farrar, Straus and Giroux.

[5] https://stephenking.com/works/novel/cujo.html

[6] https://en.wikipedia.org/wiki/Beethoven_(film)

TWO

---

# Values Are Half of Our Identity

O ur identities are a mix of our values and our behaviors. Sometimes these align and sometimes they do not. We can have an overly idealistic sense of identity if we only define ourselves in terms of our best values, but overlook the behaviors that do not match. If we are honest, we all know we espouse values or 'rules we live by' that we don't always abide by. For this reason, understanding how our framework shapes our values improves our chances of aligning them with our behavior for a fuller integration of both with our identity.

## The Formation of Our Value System and Cognitive Dissonance

Our value system comprises the beliefs, principles, and ideals that shape our decision-making and our behavior. These values are formed through a process of building correlations, drawing conclusions, and, ultimately, crafting higher-level value statements.

At the core of our value system are the correlations we establish early in life. For example, imagine a small girl growing up in a close-knit community that highly values compassion and empathy. Through her experiences and interactions, she forms a correlation between kindness and personal fulfillment. As she matures, she draws the conclusion that acting with empathy towards others leads to a sense of purpose and deep connections.

Or a child growing up in a household that highly values hard work and dedication may form a correlation between effort and success. As he matures, he may conclude that success is derived from diligent work and commitment. These conclusions then serve as the foundation for his values. The value of hard work and dedication may become integral to his value system. He perceives these values as crucial for achieving success and making decisions aligned with them, such as investing long hours or pursuing a career demanding great dedication.

It's crucial to acknowledge that values are not rigid. As we encounter new information and experiences, our values may shift or evolve. For instance, if the individual in our example encounters someone who attains success without toiling excessively, they may begin to question the belief in the value of hard work. Consequently, they may revise their values to encompass creativity or innovation over sheer effort. Values can evolve over time, either from collective value changes in our culture or more individually through intentional reflection.[7]

## Chronic Dissonance

 Now, let's delve into the negative repercussions of chronic cognitive dissonance. When individuals experience conflicting beliefs or values, it can lead to considerable inner tension and discomfort. For instance, imagine a person who strongly values environmental conservation but because of economic necessity works for a company that has a detrimental impact on the environment. This misalignment between their values and their actions creates cognitive dissonance.

Over time, chronic cognitive dissonance can have detrimental effects on mental health and overall well-being. It can lead to increased stress, anxiety, and a sense of inner conflict. In the example mentioned, the individual may struggle with feelings of guilt and frustration, knowing that their actions contradict their deeply held environmental values. Cognitive dissonance has been empirically verified, such as in a study where participants who experienced cognitive dissonance while writing an essay expressing the opposite of their true attitude showed increased activity in the anterior cingulate cortex, suggesting that the experience of cognitive dissonance produces a physiological response in the brain.[8]

Cognitive dissonance can also result in a distorted view of reality. As individuals may actively seek out information that confirms their beliefs while ignoring or dismissing evidence that contradicts them (confirmation bias). This can lead to a lack of critical thinking skills and an inability to learn and grow from new experiences and information. A recent study found that inducing cognitive dissonance in participants led to decreased prosocial behavior, indicating that cognitive dissonance can have negative effects on behavior towards others.[9] Ultimately, long-term cognitive dissonance can have negative effects on mental health, relationships, and overall well-being.

Imposter syndrome is also worth mentioning in this context. It often arises when there is a discrepancy between our perceived abilities and the expectations we have for ourselves. This dissonance can contribute to imposter syndrome, leading us to attribute our achievements to luck or external factors rather than recognizing our own capabilities. Both cognitive dissonance and imposter syndrome can result in psychological discomfort and internal conflicts. Cognitive dissonance stems from conflicting thoughts, creating stress and unease. Similarly, imposter syndrome generates an internal struggle as we try to align our perceived self-worth with our accomplishments, causing anxiety and a persistent fear of being exposed as a fraud. For instance, individuals from marginalized backgrounds may question their qualifications, believing they only obtained a job due to being a "diversity hire," while first-generation college students may struggle to recognize their academic excellence despite performing well in high school. Understanding the origins of these thoughts within our framework can contribute to a healthier self-perception.

## Our Value System on Decision-Making

Our value system significantly influences our decision-making. Values represent what we deem important, desirable, or worthy, guiding our choices and actions. Deeply ingrained in our identity, values are often shaped by our upbringing, culture, and personal experiences. Values can typically be easily identified as statements that include "should", indicating things "should" be a certain way, or "should" happen a particular way.

According to the Framework Model, our values result from the correlations and conclusions we form through our experiences and interactions with the world. Values are higher-level conclusions emerging from underlying correlations and conclusions within our framework. For instance, if we correlate the idea of not giving up with experiences of success and therefore conclude that we should strive hard, even in the face of adversity, we may develop a value of perseverance and diligence.

Values powerfully impact our decision-making and behavior, motivating us to pursue specific goals or activities and influencing our priorities and resource allocation. If we value education, for instance, we might prioritize studying and attending classes over other activities. Similarly, valuing honesty could lead us to speak truthfully, even when it is not immediately advantageous.

However, values can also create conflicts and challenges in decision-making. When we make choices that conflict with our values, we experience cognitive dissonance. When we make decisions out of alignment with our own values, it can cause serious identity issues and lead to inner turmoil, stress, and difficulty in decision-making.[10]

External factors like societal norms and expectations can influence our behaviors and sometimes conflict with our personal values. This can create tension between our personal values and society's values, leading to feelings of disconnection or disillusionment.

## The Relationship Between Our Value System and Identity

Our value system is directly linked to our internal identity. The values we hold shape how we see ourselves, who we believe we are, and our place in the world, influencing our attitudes and behaviors. These values can be defined as the principles and standards that we deem important and strive to uphold in our lives. They are formed through a combination of personal experiences, cultural and societal influences, individual priorities, and are ultimately formed through a combination of multiple conclusions built inside our framework.

Framework Theory suggests that our value system is a product of our mental model of the world and is shaped by the correlations and conclusions we draw from our experiences. Our identity, in turn, is shaped by our value system and the beliefs we hold. Our value system and identity are interconnected and constantly evolving based on experiences and interactions with the world.[11]

Our values play a significant role in shaping our sense of identity and guide our actions based on what we perceive as right or wrong. For instance, let's consider the value of not cheating on a test. When faced with the opportunity to cheat, we have a choice to either uphold our values or deviate from them. If we choose to align our behavior with our values and refrain from cheating, we reinforce our sense of self and maintain consistency. However, if we decide to cheat, a dissonance arises between our values and actions, creating internal conflict. If this dissonance remains unresolved, it can lead to feelings of guilt and potentially contribute to mental health challenges. It is crucial to address and reconcile such conflicts to maintain psychological well-being.

Resolving this dissonance is crucial for restoring inner harmony and maintaining a coherent sense of self. When faced with the gap between our values and behaviors, we have a choice: to confront it directly or to avoid it altogether. The power of this dissonance lies in its impact on our internal identity. Avoiding confrontation can lead to seemingly erratic and irrational behaviors that others may find perplexing. This avoidance may manifest as indulgence in pleasurable or painful activities or adopting a perpetually busy lifestyle as a means to temporarily escape the dissonance. While initially enjoyable and exciting to those around us, this avoidance strategy eventually reveals itself when we are alone or when confronted by caring friends or family members who see through the facade.

On the other hand, we have the option to directly confront the gap in our identity and actively seek resolution. This choice presents us with two paths: acceptance or change. If we choose acceptance, we may decide to adapt our value systems to align with our behaviors. However, this decision can have far-reaching consequences as it raises questions about subjective morality. Our behaviors are often influenced by external pressures, which can lead us to deviate from commonly accepted values within our community. By aligning our values with our behaviors, we may relieve the cognitive dissonance that plagues our identity. But in doing so, we create a new challenge: future obstacles or pressures may trigger our System 1 Response, causing us to act in ways that contradict community values. This response can have serious implications for individuals, including social ostracization and potential legal consequences, depending on the shifting values that were compromised. For example, a person who originally values honesty may feel compelled to lie under certain circumstances due to societal expectations or personal gain, thus jeopardizing their integrity and reputation.

Alternatively, we can confront our identity crisis and accept that our behaviors may not always align perfectly with our values. By acknowledging the presence of external pressures and understanding their influence on our ability to respond rationally (such as amygdala hijacking), we can restore our identity through a form of enlightenment that allows for grace and forgiveness.

This is why grace and forgiveness hold tremendous power within society. They enable individuals to move beyond their perceived failures and restore their sense of identity. This is one of the most powerful aspects of spirituality in human culture, and why spiritual health and growth is embedded in so many health frameworks. From my personal experience and journey following Christian values, I have come to recognize the profound impact of Christ's message of grace and forgiveness within these communities. Embracing the idea of absolute forgiveness can significantly aid in resolving the cognitive dissonance people carry.

The relationship between our value system and identity is complex and dynamic but becomes clearer when processed through Framework Theory. Our values shape our identity by influencing our attitudes, behaviors, and emotional responses, and guiding the choices we make. In turn, our identity can reinforce or challenge our values, depending on our experiences and interactions with the world around us. Understanding the relationship between our value system and identity is essential for developing greater self-awareness, empathy, and effective communication with others.

# References

[7] Bardi, A., & Goodwin, R. (2011). The dual route to value change: Individual processes and cultural moderators. *Journal of cross-cultural psychology, 42*(2), 271-287.

[8] Harmon-Jones, E., & Mills, J. (1999). Cognitive dissonance: Progress on a pivotal theory in social psychology. Washington, DC, US: American Psychological Association. doi: 10.1037/10396-007

[9] Müller, M., Müller, S. M., & Rösler, L. (2015). The effects of cognitive dissonance on prosocial behavior. Journal of Experimental Social Psychology, 60, 110-116. https://doi.org/10.1016/j.jesp.2015.05.007

[10] Tang, S., & Harris, L. (2015). Construing a transgression as a moral or a value violation impacts others versus self-

dehumanization. *Revue internationale de psychologie sociale,* *28*(1), 95-123.

[11] Hitlin, S. (2003). Values as the core of personal identity: Drawing links between two theories of self. *Social psychology quarterly,* 118-137.

THREE

---

# Behavior is Half of Our Identity

Our behaviors come from multiple sources. At its most basic level, we are mammals with drives and instincts. At a more complex level we are members of societies with competing pressures, norms, and goals. Our framework explains how we see and react to the world, thus influencing both aspects. Our values become high-level directives for behavior. Of course, because many of our values may have been shaped subconsciously, they are not always aligned with the version of our identity that we most desire for ourselves. First, I will discuss basic behavior and instincts and then turn to more complex forms of behavior.

## Basic Behavior and Survival Instincts

A growing body of research indicates that the primary human motivations revolve around survival and improving our chances of survival.[12] Throughout human history, our ancestors relied on the development and refinement of their frameworks to make critical decisions related to their safety and well-being. These behaviors can include our instincts to find food, shelter, and safety or our ability to adapt and respond to immediate physical threats. By drawing upon the correlations and conclusions formed within our framework, we can make decisions prioritizing our well-being and increasing our chances of survival in various situations. At one level the brain scans for signs of threat automatically,[13] but in other cases we have learned through experience to avoid certain situations, like dangerous heights. In most cases, our frameworks will guide us to avoid them and minimize the risk of harm.

Compared to most animals, humans have fewer instincts. Instincts are inborn patterns of behavior that are triggered by certain stimuli and do not require learning. While humans are born with some basic instincts, such as the instinct to suckle or grasp objects, most of our behavior is learned through socialization and experience.[14],[15] In contrast, many animals rely heavily on instincts for survival and reproduction. For example, a newborn gazelle can stand within minutes of birth and instinctively knows how to run away from predators. Similarly, birds instinctively build nests and migrate without prior experience or teaching. While humans have evolved to rely on our cognitive abilities to adapt to changing environments, our lack of strong instincts can make us more vulnerable in certain situations that we have not experienced before. For example, which berries to avoid eating because they are poisonous or which insects and snakes can cause us the most harm.

This underscores the power that our frameworks have in our survival. Because we are not born with robust innate instincts, much of our survival behavior is the result of the correlations and conclusions developed in our frameworks. While human lack of biological instinct can make us weaker in some situations, it also has the advantage of making humans far more adaptable in creating societies and ways of living in a variety of circumstances.

Most animals require a very specific habitat to survive because their instincts match their ecological environment. Humans can live nearly anywhere they have built a society or tools to navigate. In a very real sense, one can say that humans have developed institutions in place of instincts. Beyond survival, there is evidence that our morality is also developed more from our frameworks and cultural learning than biological instinct.[16]

Aside from its influence on behaviors directly related to survival, our frameworks also impact our actions and decisions that indirectly contribute to our mental and emotional well-being. These can include building social connections, pursuing hobbies or interests, and engaging in activities that promote self-esteem and personal growth. Not only do we have fight-or-flight instincts, but in times of great distress there can also be a tend-and-befriend drive to seek nurturing relationships.[17] While befriending behaviors may not have an immediate and direct impact on our physical survival, they contribute to our overall well-being, which in turn supports our ability to survive and thrive in the long run.

Our perceived needs, informed by our existing correlations and conclusions, often guide our decisions for safety, security, and social connection, which are essential components of survival. For instance, our framework may prioritize certain beliefs that contribute to our physical safety, such as avoiding dangerous situations or learning to recognize potential threats.

Similarly, our framework helps us navigate social situations, we are inherently social creatures who rely on others for support and resources. By forming connections, friends and family groups; professional alliances, trade associations, military partnerships; and institutions, schools, churches, banks, hospitals, we improve our chances of survival and well-being.

## Complex Behavior and Dark Associations

In modern society, individual's frameworks must adapt to the ever-evolving challenges and opportunities presented by technological advancements, globalization, and other contemporary factors. Our cognitive structures must be flexible enough to navigate complex environments, allowing us to make sense of the vast amounts of information and diverse perspectives we encounter daily.

*Adapting to the New World*

Technological advancements have revolutionized all aspects of our lives. From new forms of communication and information accessibility, to the fusion of science and technology, exemplified by artificial intelligence, genome editing, and other bio-tech advancements. These changes are continually challenging traditionally accepted value systems as each new breakthrough emerges. It is crucial for us to actively pursue this new information, engage in its processing, and adjust our frameworks, regardless of whether we ultimately agree or disagree with the subject matter. This principle applies to all new information we encounter: the assimilation of unfamiliar data necessitates processing, evaluation, and decision-making in light of fresh experiences and information.

Globalization presents its own set of challenges since it exposes us to a wide array of cultures, perspectives, and value systems. Our framework must be adaptable enough to accommodate these diverse viewpoints, fostering empathy and understanding while enabling us to make informed decisions in an increasingly interconnected world.

With the rapidly changing landscape of modern society, our framework becomes even more vital as we strive to understand new aspects of the world that impact how we live our lives. The core function of the framework – organizing and interpreting information to inform our conclusions, values, and decision-making processes – is crucial as we navigate the complexities of the modern world.

We can better equip ourselves to handle contemporary challenges and capitalize on new opportunities by continually updating and refining our framework. The schemas of ideas in our minds are connected to the goals we pursue.[18] Adapting our cognitive structures in response to the changing world around us is essential for our survival and well-being.

*Dark Associations*

Some behaviors, even though they may not align with our survival instincts or even our values, can trigger pleasure centers in our minds,[19] leading to correlations between those behaviors and the positive internal feelings they evoke. I call these "dark associations" because they tie physiological demands to behaviors that are counterproductive not only our individual goal to survive—they are what we identify in first-world countries as 'relativism.' These associations are assigned the term 'dark' because, in their more abstract nature, the behaviors these psychologically-mapped, physiologically-manifested desires produce are detrimental to foundations of domestication and civilization and large.

Both these correlations and behaviors can cause cognitive dissonance, which must be resolved through entering a process of consideration, and thoughtfully examining where our ideas and attitudes originated. Let's explore some real-world examples of dark associations:

1. **Substance abuse:** People may associate the temporary relief or pleasure provided by drugs or alcohol with an escape from their problems reinforcing the cycle of addiction.

2. **Compulsive gambling:** Individuals may associate the excitement of winning or the thrill of risk-taking with positive emotions leading to continued harmful behavior.

3. **Eating disorders:** People can develop associations between controlling their food intake and body weight with a sense of accomplishment, control, or self-worth perpetuating unhealthy behaviors.

4. **Self-harm:** Individuals may associate self-harming behaviors with emotional relief or a sense of control reinforcing the urge to continue engaging in destructive actions.

5. **Codependency:** In relationships, a person can develop a dark association between pleasing others and feeling loved or valued which can lead  to unhealthy levels of self-sacrifice and an inability to establish personal boundaries..

6. **Maladaptive Sexual Attraction:** A person might develop an unhealthy attraction to others through correlations between affection and hormonal sexual impulses during volatile stages of development or other life events.

7. **Identity Crisis:** A person may struggle with their sense of who they are due to false correlations formed in early childhood, classical conditioning, social influence, or reinforcement. Trying on new behaviors and roles can feel freeing, but also can be damaging if they are erratic

or inconsistent with the laws of nature or biological, objective reality.

In each of these examples, a behavior or belief that is ultimately harmful or maladaptive becomes reinforced through the activation of pleasure centers or the meeting of emotional needs.

Over time, as individuals attach these maladaptive behaviors to pleasure, they may become more likely to use confirmation bias to rationalize their actions. This cognitive bias leads them to focus on information that supports their beliefs and behaviors while dismissing or ignoring contradictory evidence. As a result, they may construct narratives that justify their actions and convince themselves that these behaviors have positive outcomes. For example, even though they are drinking to excess every night, they may tell themselves they deserve to have a few drinks to relax after a hard day or that they are more sociable when inebriated. Of course, they wake up with a hangover and are nervous to review whatever texts they may have sent while blacked out. This adds to the stress and anxiety they feel, leading them to feel even more in need of a few drinks the following night.

In the process, they may create a feedback loop that further reinforces their dark associations making it increasingly difficult to break free from these patterns. This underscores the importance of developing self-awareness, critical thinking skills, and emotional intelligence. By recognizing and challenging these biases and assumptions, individuals can begin to dismantle the dark associations that have taken root in their lives and make healthier choices that align with their true values and goals.

In clinical settings, when dark associations become chronic and long-lasting, therapists will often diagnose someone with borderline personality disorder[20] which impacts how a person thinks and feels about themselves and others. It is characterized by pervasive instability in interpersonal relationships, self-image, and emotions as well as impulsive and self-destructive behaviors. People who suffer from borderline personality disorder can have an intense fear of abandonment, shifting goals and values, mood swings, ongoing feelings of emptiness, and are known to sabotage important relationships or jobs.

A therapist can help an individual work through this by posing exploratory questions that lead them through their framework; questions they may not otherwise ask or even intentionally avoid. In some circumstances, they can also produce similar outcomes by entering into a state of consideration and processing the false correlations and conclusions held in their framework. This process is also called emotional self-regulation[21] and happens when we intentionally work through understanding how to tolerate the uncomfortable feelings that are an inevitable part of life.

The challenge we may sometimes face when assessing our framework alone is that we may not possess the underlying knowledge needed to facilitate a reformation of our upper-level conclusions. At times we all need to seek additional knowledge and outside perspectives in order to challenge our existing beliefs and come to new conclusions. This is the value of an educated, objective third party who can help us get the information we need to alter our framework and reframe our understanding of the world.

Maturity and the ability to control the impulses uncomfortable feelings create is demonstrated by the capacity to confront emotional, social, and cognitive challenges in the environment with patience and thoughtfulness. That is the fundamental purpose of examining our frameworks to systematically identify false correlations and the dark associations they can lead to, so we can lead healthier and more fulfilling lives.

## **Table 1.** Components of Identity and Their Expression

| Components of Identity | Values | Behaviors |
| --- | --- | --- |
| Beliefs | Reflect personal principles and ideals | Manifest through actions and choices |
| Priorities | Determine what is important in life | Evident in the allocation of time and resources |
| Morals | Dictate right and wrong | Reflected in ethical decisions |
| Goals | Represent desired aspirations | Pursued actively through efforts |
| Interests | Reflect personal passions | Engaged in through participation |
| Attitudes | Shape overall outlook and perspective | Displayed in interactions with others |
| Relationships | Guided by values such as trust, respect, and loyalty | Demonstrated through interactions and commitments |

*This table highlights how values shape human identity by linking internal components—beliefs, priorities, morals, goals, interests, attitudes, and relationships—to outward behaviors. It shows the complexity of how values inform choices, guide interactions, and manifest in everyday life as the rules we live by.*

# References

[12] Stevens, L. E., & Fiske, S. T. (1995). Motivation and cognition in social life: A social survival perspective. *Social cognition, 13*(3), 189-214.

[13] Larson, C. L., Aronoff, J., Sarinopoulos, I. C., & Zhu, D. C. (2009). Recognizing threat: A simple geometric shape activates neural circuitry for threat detection. *Journal of cognitive neuroscience, 21*(8), 1523-1535.

[14] Buss, D. M. (2015). Evolutionary psychology: The new science of the mind (5th ed.). Psychology Press.

[15] Geary, D. C. (2005). The origin of mind: Evolution of brain, cognition, and general intelligence. American Psychological Association.

[16] Haidt, J. (2001). The emotional dog and its rational tail: A social intuitionist approach to moral judgment. Psychological Review, 108(4), 814-834.

[17] Taylor, S. E. (2012). Tend and befriend theory. *Handbook of theories of social psychology, 1*, 32-49.

[18] Cooper, R. P., & Shallice, T. (2006). Hierarchical schemas and goals in the control of sequential behavior.

[19] Berridge, K. C., & Kringelbach, M. L. (2015). Pleasure systems in the brain. Neuron, 86(3), 646-664.

[20]                https://www.mayoclinic.org/diseases-conditions/borderline-personality-disorder/symptoms-causes/syc-20370237

[21]    https://www.verywellmind.com/how-you-can-practice-self-regulation-4163536

FOUR

---

# Social Contexts Influence Us

The Framework Model is a powerful tool for understanding the development of our identity and organizing our thoughts. However, individual frameworks' reliance on external information can also make them vulnerable to manipulation, false correlations, confirmation bias, and cognitive dissonance. Social influence can have a significant impact on our frameworks, leading to the acceptance of false conclusions and the formation of harmful values that threaten the stability of society.

Experiences with community[22] and culture[23] play a crucial role in shaping a person's identity and values. Community norms and expectations create social pressure for people as they strive for acceptance in their communities and ultimately help shape that individual's framework. For instance, a person's family, schoolteachers, counselors, or other influential roles models may hold certain beliefs about other ethnicities, gender roles, religion, or politics, which may conflict with objective reality, and they may be passed down during a child's formative years. These beliefs established at the core of one's framework will become deeply ingrained in the child's sense of self and present themselves as core values later in life.

It is also important to note that a lack of exposure to diverse experiences and viewpoints within one's family or community can contribute to the development of false correlations and ultimately hinder the formation of a more nuanced and inclusive belief system.[24] Lack of exposure to diverse experiences leaves room in our framework for objectively false correlations to be created.

The impact of social and environmental factors on the development of conclusions and values is multifaceted. Our social and cultural contexts shape our perceptions of reality and influences the formation of our framework. Factors such as social norms,[25] media exposure,[26] and peer pressure[27] all contribute to the intricate tapestry of our conclusions and values.

## Examples of Social Influence and Negative Outcomes

*Fear-mongering, Propaganda and Groupthink*

In order to improve our chances of physical and social survival, we understand that we need to live in community with others. When others around us begin to act out of fear or even simply change their behavior patterns, it triggers a primal response[28] that causes us to shift our behavior to align with theirs.[29] This cognitive/behavioral mechanism helps us stay connected or even bond with those around us, which can prevent negative consequences like exclusion and ostracism.[30] The larger the group of people modifying their behavior, the greater the pressure on us to change our behavior. We may be motivated by the fear of missing out, also known as FOMO. This normative group influence is sometimes referred to as "social proof."[31]

When we observe others around us acting out of fear, it can undermine our ability to reason effectively, and we may find ourselves resorting more to instinctual responses rather than rational thinking. However, once the initial hormonal response subsides and our capacity for rational thought is restored, we may experience a cognitive dissonance known as "post-decision dissonance" if our actions were not in alignment with our values. This dissonance can arise even if we are uncertain whether our decisions truly reflected our values.

The consequences of social influence can be devastating and catastrophic as seen in the cases of Nazi Germany and the Salem Witch Trials. In both instances, social influence was used to shape a population's beliefs and behaviors leading them to conform to societal norms and expectations. This was possible due to a vulnerability in that society's framework linked to their primal survival instinct.

In Nazi Germany, social influence was used to indoctrinate citizens with Nazi ideology, encouraging them to support the regime's policies and participate in its atrocities, such as the Holocaust. This resulted in widespread persecution, discrimination, and the deaths of millions of innocent people.

Similarly, in the Salem Witch Trials, social influence was used to fuel paranoia and suspicion, causing hundreds of innocent people to be accused and persecuted for witchcraft. The trials resulted in the execution of many people and traumatized the community. These tragedies serve as reminders of the power of social influence, the importance of critical thinking, and rational decision-making in times of crisis. They illustrate that blindly following authority and succumbing to groupthink can have dire consequences.

The speed at which we process new information and react based on existing beliefs is truly remarkable. This is particularly evident in the bank runs in 2023 that led to the rapid demise of Silicon Valley Bank, Signature Bank, and First Republic Bank in a matter of days as word of their instability spread rapidly through social media and depositors quickly withdrew funds.[32] Or consider the toilet paper shortage of 2020, where panic buying quickly spread through social influence.[33] In both cases, false beliefs and misinformation led to a rush to withdraw money from banks or hoard toilet paper, despite no real shortage or instability. Such social contagions can have devastating economic consequences, destabilizing entire sectors and leading to potential collapse. The impact of social influence on the economy is not limited to these events, since false beliefs or misinformation about a particular product or industry can negatively impact trade and erode the foundations of civilized society. Propaganda, peer pressure, and groupthink can all contribute to the manipulation of individuals and societies, distorting reality and creating a ripple effect that can be difficult to control. It is essential to be aware of the power of social influence and to approach new information with critical thinking and rational decision-making.

*Transgenderism*

Similarly, societal norms and expectations surrounding sexual relationships, gender identity, and mental health can shape our understanding and values in these areas. However, if these norms and expectations are inaccurate or harmful, the propagation of false or harmful conclusions can contribute to mental health crises, societal tensions, and undermine individual well-being. Therefore, it is essential to critically examine the impact of societal norms and expectations on our frameworks and challenge any false or harmful conclusions that may emerge.

In some cases, even well-intentioned organizations can contribute to the spread of harmful conclusions and misinformation. For example, the **American Psychological Association (APA)** and other professional bodies may change definitions and remove disorders from their diagnostic manuals in response to social movements or pressure from interest groups.[34] While these changes may be aimed at reducing stigma and promoting inclusivity, they can inadvertently lead to harmful outcomes for individuals with mental disorders related to their framework, such as gender confusion and transgenderism.

By altering diagnostic criteria and definitions, these organizations may inadvertently contribute to the normalization of conditions that warrant further investigation and treatment. This can leave affected individuals without the necessary support and resources, which may lead to a worsening of their mental health and a reduced quality of life. Additionally, these changes can create confusion among mental health professionals who may struggle to provide appropriate care and guidance to individuals grappling with these complex issues.

Mental health professionals may encounter legal obstacles in providing adequate care for individuals grappling with distorted realities. Political figures and legislators, driven by motivations that may not align with societal well-being but who are influenced by political strategists exploiting groupthink and confirmation bias, may employ various communication tactics and propaganda to change society. These strategies lead to the implementation of legislation that hinders essential healthcare approaches needed to assist those suffering from false correlations and conclusions.

Additionally, it is crucial to consider how these distorted beliefs become deeply ingrained through confirmation bias within personal circles. Friends, family members, celebrities, and news anchors, even if they do not genuinely endorse or agree with these distorted realities, may "fake it" to avoid confrontations or face the risk of social isolation. Despite their actual values not aligning with such ideas, mass media and social platforms create a false perception of a popular movement supporting fringe concepts like the normalization of identity crises such as transgenderism, human-animal sexual relationships, and even adult-child sexual relationships under the guise of the "Minor Attracted Persons" movement.[35]

To counteract the negative consequences of such changes, it is essential for mental health organizations and professionals to maintain a commitment to evidence-based practice, continually updating their understanding of mental health disorders in light of new unbiased research and findings. This includes critically examining the impact of societal norms and expectations on the diagnostic process and ensuring that individuals receive appropriate care and support to address their unique mental health needs. By doing so, these organizations can help prevent the erosion of our framework due to misinformation and promote better outcomes for individuals facing mental health challenges.

*Bad Information Can Spread Rapidly*

In today's world, where communication is instant and spreads rapidly, massive cultural shifts can begin in a single news cycle. This can have a negative impact on mental health for individuals who lack knowledge, education, and a broader perspective and may be more susceptible to external influence. On a small scale, in 2016, a false conspiracy theory called "Pizzagate" circulated online, claiming that a Washington D.C. pizzeria was a front for a child sex trafficking ring involving high-ranking politicians.[36] The false claim led to an armed man entering the pizzeria and firing shots, fortunately, no one was injured.

On a broader scale, the dissemination of misinformation and government-endorsed propaganda surrounding the COVID-19 virus and its transmission was widespread on social media platforms. Initially, reports suggested that the virus originated from a meat market and was spread by bats depicted in various media outlets. However, recent investigations have raised concerns about the origins of the virus, indicating the possibility of a potential leak from a government-funded lab in China rather than a natural evolution from bats.[37] Congressional oversight committees and the National Institute of Allergy and Infectious Diseases are currently examining this hypothesis of a potential lead from a Chinese funded lab related to gain-of-function research. These developments challenge the accuracy of previously presented information and highlight the impact of misinformation on the public's understanding of the pandemic's severity. By withholding the lab theory, Americans were potentially deprived of vital information to assess the full spectrum of threats to their safety, such as potential bioterrorism or attempts to disrupt the U.S. election, despite the lack of conclusive evidence supporting such claims. It is essential to recognize the influence of this suppressed information on public perception and to acknowledge that the narrative surrounding the virus's origins is evolving as new investigations unfold.

## The Basic Problem

Social and environmental factors play a critical role in shaping our conclusions and values. They create a complex web of experiences that inform our understanding of the world. When we encounter new information, we evaluate it against our existing framework. We either incorporating it into our belief system or dismissing it as false. This process fosters confidence in our worldview but can also render our framework rigid and resistant to change. Two main problems arise when social influence leads us to mistaken ideas.

**False correlations** occur when we erroneously identify connections between unrelated events or pieces of information. These false correlations can lead us to form inaccurate conclusions, resulting in misguided decisions that may hinder our ability to thrive or even threaten our well-being.

**Cognitive dissonance** arises when we hold conflicting conclusions or values within our framework. This internal conflict can lead to mental stress and confusion, impairing our decision-making abilities and potentially causing us to make choices that are detrimental to our thriving.

Cognitive dissonance can have utility. At times, new information may challenge our current beliefs and may lead to cognitive dissonance. This dissonance can provoke introspection, potentially resulting in a shift in our conclusions and values. However, since this process is mentally taxing and uncomfortable, people often resist changing their beliefs, even when confronted with persuasive evidence. They leave their false correlations and cognitive dissonance intact by either justifying it or avoiding introspection altogether with diversions. Long-term cognitive dissonance left in place becomes toxic to our functioning and well-being.

Furthermore, our social and environmental contexts can also affect how we address cognitive dissonance. For example, tight versus loose cultures is a concept in social psychology that refers to the degree to which social norms and rules are enforced in a society.[38], [39] Tight cultures have strong norms and punish deviant behavior, while loose cultures have weaker norms and tolerate more deviance. Questioning authority and challenging traditional beliefs might be encouraged in loose cultures, while in tight cultures, conformity and respect for authority may be prioritized. These cultural differences can affect a wide range of behaviors and attitudes including political beliefs, social attitudes, and individual personality traits. These cultural differences can shape how individuals respond to new information, ultimately impacting the formation of their conclusions and values and how they deal with cognitive dissonance.

## Resisting Negative Social Influence

To safeguard our framework from the detrimental effects of social influence and manipulation, we must be proactive in recognizing and challenging the biases and cognitive dissonance that can compromise our understanding of reality. This involves:

1. **Diverse Viewpoints:** Actively seeking alternative perspectives and information to counteract confirmation bias and encourage a more open-minded approach to interpreting and organizing information within the Framework.

2. **Critical Thinking:** Developing critical thinking skills and healthy skepticism to assess the veracity and reliability of information, particularly when it comes from sources that may have vested interests or biases.

3. **Self-Reflection:** Engaging in self-reflection and introspection to identify and address instances of cognitive dissonance, promoting greater self-awareness and alignment between our conclusions, values, and actions.

By recognizing the fragility of the framework and actively working to mitigate its vulnerabilities, we can more effectively utilize the framework as a tool for personal growth and development. This will ultimately enable us to foster a more accurate understanding of ourselves and the world around us and protecting our societies from the devastating consequences of false conclusions and harmful values.

Resisting negative social influence can be a challenging task, but it is essential to ensure that our beliefs and values align with reality and are not manipulated by external forces. One effective way to resist negative social influence is to develop critical thinking skills and actively question information that is presented to us. By analyzing sources, checking facts, and considering alternative perspectives, we can become less susceptible to manipulation and false conclusions. It is also important to be aware of our biases, how they may impact our decision-making, and to seek out diverse opinions and viewpoints to broaden our understanding of a topic. Additionally, it can be helpful to surround ourselves with people who share our values and support our growth, rather than those who may be pushing us towards negative behaviors or beliefs. By actively resisting negative social influence, we can protect ourselves and contribute to the creation of a healthier, more informed society.

# References

[22] Howes, C. (2010). A model for studying socialization in early childhood education and care settings. In *Peer relationships in early childhood education and care* (pp. 29-40). Routledge.

[23] Harwood, R. L., Schoelmerich, A., Ventura-Cook, E., Schulze, P. A., & Wilson, S. P. (1996). Culture and class influences on Anglo and Puerto Rican mothers' beliefs regarding long-term socialization goals and child behavior. *Child Development, 67*(5), 2446-2461.

[24] Johnson, S. M., & Lollar, X. L. (2002). Diversity policy in higher education: the impact of college students' exposure to diversity on cultural awareness and political participation. *Journal of education Policy, 17*(3), 305-320.

[25] d'Adda, G., Dufwenberg, M., Passarelli, F., & Tabellini, G. (2020). Social norms with private values: Theory and experiments. *Games and Economic Behavior, 124*, 288-304.

[26] Héricourt, J., & Spielvogel, G. (2014). Beliefs, media exposure and policy preferences on immigration: Evidence from Europe. *Applied Economics, 46*(2), 225-239.

[27] Lashbrook, J. T. (2000). Fitting in: Exploring the emotional dimension of adolescent peer pressure. *Adolescence*, *35*(140), 747.

[28] Hariri AR, Tessitore A, Mattay VS, Fera F, Weinberger DR. The amygdala response to emotional stimuli: a comparison of faces and scenes. Neuroimage. 2002 Sep;17(1):317-23. doi: 10.1006/nimg.2002.1179. PMID: 12482086.

[29] Genschow O, Klomfar S, d'Haene I, Brass M. Mimicking and anticipating others' actions is linked to Social Information Processing. PLoS One. 2018 Mar 28;13(3):e0193743. doi: 10.1371/journal.pone.0193743. PMID: 29590127; PMCID: PMC5873994.

[30] Eisenberger, N. I., Lieberman, M. D., & Williams, K. D. (2003). Does rejection hurt? An fMRI study of social exclusion. Science, 302(5643), 290-292.

[31] Venema TAG, Kroese FM, Benjamins JS, de Ridder DTD. When in Doubt, Follow the Crowd? Responsiveness to Social Proof Nudges in the Absence of Clear Preferences. Front Psychol. 2020 Jun 18;11:1385. doi: 10.3389/fpsyg.2020.01385. PMID: 32655456; PMCID: PMC7325907.

[32] https://www.fdic.gov/bank/historical/bank/bfb2023.html

[33] https://www.washingtonpost.com/national/coronavirus-toilet-paper-shortage-panic/2020/04/07/1fd30e92-75b5-11ea-87da-77a8136c1a6d_story.html

[34] Wakefield, J. C. (2013). DSM-5: An overview of changes and controversies. *Clinical Social Work Journal, 41*, 139-154.

[35] https://en.wikipedia.org/wiki/Minor-attracted_person

[36] Tani, M. (2016, December 4). Gunman motivated by 'Pizzagate' conspiracy theory arrested, D.C. police say. NBC News. https://www.nbcnews.com/news/us-news/gunman-motivated-pizzagate-conspiracy-theory-arrested-d-c-police-say-n691401

[37]https://oversight.house.gov/release/covid-origins-hearing-wrap-up-facts-science-evidence-point-to-a-wuhan-lab-leak%ef%bf%bc/

[38] Gelfand, M. (2019). Rule makers, rule breakers: Tight and loose cultures and the secret signals that direct our lives. Scribner.

[39] Gelfand, M. J., Raver, J. L., Nishii, L., Leslie, L. M., Lun, J., Lim, B. C., ... & Yamaguchi, S. (2011). Differences between tight and loose cultures: A 33-nation study. *science, 332*(6033), 1100-1104.

FIVE

---

# *Early Experiences Affect Us*

Early experiences play a critical role in shaping our conclusions,[40] values,[41] and identity[42] through our framework. During our early years, we are particularly vulnerable to external influences, as we have very few existing correlations and conclusions to make sense of the world around us. As a result, the conclusions we draw during this time become the building blocks of our framework and have a lasting impact on our conclusions, values, and identity.

For example, a child growing up in an environment where their parents hold certain conclusions and values is likely to adopt those same conclusions and values as their own.[43] This is because the child's framework is still in its formative stages and is heavily influenced by external factors. As the child experiences new situations and information, they use their existing framework to interpret and make sense of these experiences, reinforcing and expanding upon their existing conclusions and values.

However, not all early experiences are positive or supportive of healthy development. For example, a child who experiences trauma or abuse may form conclusions about the world and themselves that are based on fear, mistrust, or low self-worth.[44] These conclusions can become deeply ingrained in the child's framework and can have a significant impact on their conclusions, values, and identity as they grow older.

## Early Development and Negative vs Positive Outcomes

How our framework is formed when we are young can lead to a range of outcomes. Early experiences that lead to false correlations, cognitive dissonance, and can ultimately contribute to the development of mental health disorders later in life. False correlations, formed when a person tries to make sense of the world around them by linking unrelated information, can result in the development of false conclusions. These beliefs, which are often formed early in life through observation and imitating family members, can lead to cognitive dissonance when presented with contradictory information or objective reality. Cognitive dissonance, in turn, could be linked as a root cause for issues like anxiety, depression, bipolar disorder, and obsessive-compulsive disorder (OCD).

These factors can contribute to the development of extreme or polarized thinking patterns. For example, if a person has a false belief that they are always right or that the world is always against them, this can create a pattern of extreme thinking that is characteristic of bipolar disorder, including signs of grandiosity and megalomania.[45]

While early experiences can contribute to the development of mental health disorders, they can also have positive effects on a person's identity and self-esteem.[46] Supportive families and communities can instill a sense of belonging and foster a growth mindset, allowing individuals to believe in their potential and develop positive values.

For example, a child growing up in a family that values education and hard work is more likely to develop a positive framework around these values. They may draw correlations between working hard and achieving success, leading them to form the conclusion that they should prioritize their education and put effort into their schoolwork. This value of education and hard work can become a part of their identity and lead to positive outcomes later in life, such as academic success or career advancement.

Similarly, a child growing up in a community that values kindness and empathy is more likely to develop a positive framework around these values. They may draw a correlation between being kind to others and forming positive relationships, leading them to form the conclusion that they should treat others with empathy and respect. This value of kindness and empathy can become a part of their identity and lead to positive outcomes later in life, such as strong relationships and a sense of community.

In these examples, the positive values are formed through correlations and conclusions drawn from early experiences. These become a part of the person's framework. This positive framework can lead to positive outcomes and contribute to a person's sense of identity and self-esteem.

Family, culture, and community in shaping a person's identity and values cannot be overlooked. While early experiences can have negative effects on mental health through the formation of false beliefs and cognitive dissonance, they can also have positive effects through the development of a growth mindset and positive values.[47] It is important to recognize the impact of early experiences and work to promote healthy development in children and adolescents. Parents and other trusted adults play a crucial role in shaping our early development by providing us with information about the world, which serves as the foundation for our future conclusions and values. However, parents may unintentionally pass on incorrect information or false beliefs, which may lead to forming misguided conclusions.

The same can be true of social and environmental factors outside of our families of origin. This is partly due to our tendency to misinterpret information, influenced through the lens in which we view the world. Our brains are not evolved to be objective observers, but are rather pattern seekers, to maximize our survival[48]. For instance, when our ancestors heard the bushes rustling, they assumed there must be a predator and prepared accordingly. Although they could have objectively determined that the probability of a predator was low, they would only have to be wrong once to fail to pass their genes along. False negatives can be deadly, but false positives, assuming it was a predator when it was only the wind, were less costly. Thus, we are wired to overinterpret patterns and over attribute phenomena due to cognitive biases.

Much discussion has gone into the nature versus nurture debate, or the influence of socialization on who we become versus our genetics. This chapter takes a slightly different angle to distinguish between nature and culture. It explores how our upbringings, as well as the cultural influences that surround us, shape our conclusions and values. We are highly susceptible to both, largely due to cognitive biases which will be discussed in greater detail at the end of the chapter.

## Parental Influences on Conclusions and Values

When we receive a conclusion from a trusted source, such as our parents, we enter a state of consideration, seeking correlations to support their conclusion through confirmation bias. We may desire to believe they are right and, as a result, work to validate their conclusions. This process stems from a survival instinct, as we depend on parents and other trusted adults for protection and care. As children, we are completely dependent on our parents and learn that it is in our best interests to do and believe what they say. This is well and good when they are telling us to eat our vegetables, avoid playing in traffic, and to avoid running with knives. But as we mature we have a difficult time sorting these kinds of lessons from other conclusions that may not be so directly beneficial for us, or at least not obviously so. For example, when they tell us which careers to pursue, how to treat our romantic partners, or what political perspectives to take. Nevertheless, we tend to want to believe our parents, at least until we reach a later stage of maturity, and, even then, not everyone takes the time to critique the conclusions and values passed on to them.

As we grow and develop, the conclusions drawn from early experiences become deeply embedded in our framework constituting the core of our value system. These formative experiences and their resulting conclusions and values can significantly impact our future identity and perspective. Over time, as we face new information and experiences, we may begin to question and reassess these conclusions and values. This reassessment is *consideration* or System 2 Thinking. This can lead to shifts in our framework and, ultimately to our understanding and perspective of the world. Parents hold a significant responsibility in shaping their children's beliefs and values as they impart fundamental correlations and conclusions about the world. From a young age, parents teach their children simple associations such as the correlation between colors and their names, letters and their sounds, and object names and their corresponding objects. These early teachings lay the foundation for cognitive development and language acquisition. Parents serve as the primary influencers introducing their children to the fundamental correlations that form the building blocks of understanding the world around them.

While this can be beneficial in many cases, there are instances where parental influence can negatively impact a child's framework due to improper correlations and conclusions.

For example, consider a situation where a parent, Amy, has an irrational fear of using the subway due to a traumatic childhood experience. When Amy was six, she was on the subway with her mother when the train hit something on the tracks and abruptly halted, the lights went out briefly and all the passengers fell to the ground. After the lights came back on and the passengers regained their composure, Amy's mother realized her purse had been stolen during the chaos. The incident was terrifying for Amy and she said to her mother, "I never want to ride on a train again."

Due to her traumatic experience, and as a result of her young mind, Amy concluded that because this train caused her pain and fear, all trains and subways are too dangerous to use.

Amy was too young to have information regarding the benefit of trains and objectively the low likelihood of that situation happening again. As a result, Amy carried this conclusion with her into her adult life, never reconciling the past or reconsidering the conclusions she had through her more experienced lens. Wanting to protect her own child, Amy communicates this belief to her daughter Mary from an early age even though they live in New York City where the subway is an essential mode of transportation. Mary trusts her mother as a reliable source of information and accepts this belief as true, forming her own negative views about trains and subways.

As Mary grows up, she observes that her mother avoids the subway as often as possible, and when Amy must use it, she becomes anxious. Amy also highlights every news report of train crashes and subway robberies to Mary, further reinforcing her belief in the inherent danger of trains and subways. As Mary matures, she may also seek out stories that confirm her Mother's belief while ignoring countless instances where trains and subways safely transport passengers to their destinations. This kind of selective acceptance of information is called confirmation bias.

The impact of Amy's unfounded fear of using the subway extends beyond her and her daughter Mary's personal lives even affecting their financial outlook. Throughout Mary's life, she has been conditioned to avoid trains and subways due to her mother's irrational fear. Consequently, Mary incurs additional expenses from relying on taxis or alternative modes of transportation, leading to a considerable financial burden. The accumulated costs of taxi fees, loss of productivity, and missed job opportunities over the course of her life cannot be underestimated. This all stems from this seemingly insignificant belief passed down by her mother. The ripple effect of irrational beliefs can have far-reaching consequences affecting not only personal experiences but also the financial well-being of individuals and their future opportunities.

In this example, Amy's conclusion based on her personal experience has led to the formation of an irrational fear of trains and subways in her child's framework. Mary's belief system has been shaped by her parent's perspective rather than an objective evaluation of the actual risk posed by trains and subways.

It is essential for parents to be aware of how their own biases and experiences can affect their children's belief formation.

The consequences of generational ignorance such as the foundation Amy created for Mary can be far-reaching and devastating. Mary's negative belief about trains and subways, instilled by her mother, shapes her worldview and decision-making processes. Beyond fees and missed job opportunities, she may also miss out on educational opportunities, avoiding universities or programs that are only accessible by public transportation. Moreover, Mary's limited exposure to efficient and cost-effective modes of transportation may hinder her ability to explore new areas, discover diverse cultures, and expand her horizons. The perpetuation of unfounded beliefs from one generation to the next can create a cycle of ignorance, limiting opportunities and perpetuating narrow perspectives that hinder personal growth and societal progress.

Encouraging open dialogue, promoting critical thinking, and exposing children to a variety of perspectives can help foster a more balanced and accurate framework, allowing children to form their own conclusions based on objective information and experiences.

## References

[40] Andreas, J. B., & Watson, M. W. (2009). Moderating effects of family environment on the association between children's aggressive beliefs and their aggression trajectories from childhood to adolescence. *Development and psychopathology*, *21*(1), 189-205.

[41] Fouad, N. A., Cotter, E. W., Fitzpatrick, M. E., Kantamneni, N., Carter, L., & Bernfeld, S. (2010). Development and

validation of the family influence scale. *Journal of Career Assessment, 18*(3), 276-291.

[42] Streamer, L., & Seery, M. D. (2015). Who am I? The interactive effect of early family experiences and self-esteem in predicting self-clarity. *Personality and Individual Differences, 77*, 18-21.

[43] Murphey, D. A. (1992). Constructing the child: Relations between parents' beliefs and child outcomes. *Developmental review, 12*(2), 199-232.

[44] Lubit, R., Rovine, D., DeFrancisci, L., & Eth, S. (2003). Impact of trauma on children. *Journal of Psychiatric Practice, 9*(2), 128-138.

[45] Grande, I., Berk, M., Birmaher, B., & Vieta, E. (2016). Bipolar disorder. The Lancet, 387(10027), 1561-1572.

[46] AlShawi, A. F., & Lafta, R. K. (2015). Relation between childhood experiences and adults' self-esteem: A sample from Baghdad. *Qatar Medical Journal, 2014*(2), 14.

[47] Haimovitz, K., & Dweck, C. S. (2017). The origins of children's growth and fixed mindsets: New research and a new proposal. *Child development, 88*(6), 1849-1859.

[48] Andersen, M. (2019). Predictive coding in agency detection. Religion, Brain & Behavior, 9(1), 65-84.

SIX

---

# *Cognitive Biases Mislead Us*

C ognitive biases significantly influence the formation of conclusions and values by affecting the correlations we draw from new information. When we encounter new information, we often evaluate it based on our existing framework of beliefs. We are more likely to accept new information as true and incorporate it into our belief system if it aligns with our existing framework. Conversely, if the new information conflicts with our existing framework, we may be more likely to reject it or seek out alternative interpretations that align with our beliefs.

## Basic Types of Biases

This process is heavily influenced by cognitive biases, which are mental shortcuts and heuristics that can lead to errors in judgment. Some examples of cognitive biases include:

1. **Confirmation bias:**[49] The tendency to seek out information that confirms our existing beliefs and ignore information that contradicts them.

2. **Availability heuristic:**[50] The tendency to overestimate the likelihood of events based on the ease with which they come to mind.

3. **Anchoring bias:**[51] The tendency to rely too heavily on an initial piece of information when making decisions.

Cognitive biases can hinder our ability to make objective and rational decisions that contribute to our survival. These biases can lead us to overlook important information, misinterpret situations, or make impulsive decisions based on limited or flawed data. For example, when confirmation bias causes us to focus only on evidence that supports our pre-existing conclusions, it leads to an inaccurate understanding of our environment and, consequently, a diminished capacity to make informed decisions.[52] Similarly, when anchoring causes us to rely too heavily on an initial piece of information that is irrelevant or inaccurate, we make less healthy decisions.[53]

Our inclination to rely on cognitive biases as a survival mechanism is deeply rooted in our evolutionary history. These biases serve to protect our existing belief systems, which have helped us navigate and survive in the world thus far. We naturally gravitate toward information that reinforces our preconceived notions, shielding our framework from potential external influences that might mislead or lead us astray from what we perceive as a safe path. We may even consciously or unconsciously avoid new information if we deem that the benefit of learning and understanding it do not outweigh the advantages of maintaining our current belief systems. Additionally, we may shy away from new information if we anticipate that it could inflict significant mental pain and anguish.

Denial serves as a defense mechanism in various situations and illustrates the influence of cognitive biases on our perception of reality. For instance, when faced with evidence of a partner's infidelity, individuals may enter a state of denial, unwilling to accept the truth and instead clinging to the belief of their partner's faithfulness. This denial shields them from the emotional pain and upheaval that acknowledging the infidelity would bring.

Similarly, individuals struggling with addiction may deny the extent of their dependency and avoiding the distressing realization of the negative consequences it has on their life. Denial acts as a protective barrier, granting temporary respite from the immediate psychological distress associated with acknowledging their addictive behaviors. Additionally, when receiving a serious medical diagnosis, individuals may initially deny or downplay its severity as a way to cope with the overwhelming emotional distress. Denial offers a temporary shield from immediate anguish allowing them to gradually process the information. These examples emphasize the role of denial as a self-preservation mechanism, but it is important to confront these truths for personal growth, well-being, and an accurate understanding of the world.

Cognitive biases can interact with one's framework in complex ways, leading to the formation of beliefs that are inconsistent or contradictory. For example, if a person has a pre-existing conclusion stored in their framework, they may be more likely to accept or reject new information based on whether it aligns with or contradicts that conclusion. Even if conflicting knowledge is presented by a trusted source, a person may be more likely to find or build correlations that support their existing beliefs rather than challenge them. In social psychology, this is often discussed as the difference between assimilation and accommodation. Assimilation involves fitting new information into an existing schema without altering it substantially. This means that individuals may only incorporate new information that is consistent with their existing beliefs and ignore or reject information that is inconsistent with their schemas. Accommodation, on the other hand, involves modifying or creating new schemas to incorporate new information that is not consistent with one's existing ideas. This process may require individuals to revise their beliefs and may be more cognitively demanding than assimilation. Many people avoid this cognitive labor, whether it be due to a lack of awareness or intentionally avoiding internal conflict, but ultimately the pain of not addressing cognitive dissonance becomes far greater than the work to remedy it.

## Positive Emotions and False Correlations

Positive emotions, while generally beneficial for our mental well-being, can also influence our susceptibility to false correlations. When we are in a positive emotional state, we may be more inclined to accept information without questioning its validity or seeking corroborating evidence.[54] This can lead to the formation of beliefs that may not necessarily be based on objective facts or sound reasoning.

The role of positive emotions in shaping our values is significant. Positive emotions can make us more open to new ideas, more willing to engage with others, and more likely to see the best in people and situations. However, it's essential to recognize that these emotions can also make us vulnerable to accepting false correlations or misleading information. Striking a balance between maintaining a positive outlook and exercising a healthy level of skepticism and critical thinking is crucial for developing a robust and accurate framework.

A real-world example of the impact of positive emotions on our perceptions and conclusions can be seen in the "halo effect." [55] The halo effect is a cognitive bias where our positive feelings about a person or thing can lead us to overgeneralize these positive attributes to other unrelated areas. For instance, if we have a favorable impression of a celebrity, we might be more likely to believe in their opinions on political or social issues, even if they lack expertise in those areas. This tendency to form false correlations based on positive emotions can lead to the development of misguided conclusions and values within our framework.

A relevant study supporting this concept is the 1977 experiment by Nisbett and Wilson, which demonstrated that people's judgments of a lecturer's competence were significantly influenced by their initial impressions of the lecturer's physical attractiveness.[56] The positive emotions evoked by the lecturer's appearance led participants to form false correlations between their attractiveness and their competence, over-assuming their skill level simply because they were easy on the eyes. This "halo effect" [57] showcases the powerful influence of positive emotions on our perceptions and conclusions.

Another example that highlights the influence of positive emotions on our perceptions and conclusions is the phenomenon of catfishing. Catfishing refers to the act of creating a deceptive online persona from who they really are to establish false relationships or manipulate others.

In online dating or social media interactions, individuals may encounter someone who presents themselves with an attractive profile, engaging personality, and appealing qualities. The positive emotions evoked by this virtual connection can cloud judgment and lead to a suspension of skepticism. People may be more inclined to believe the information presented by the catfisher, even if there are inconsistencies or red flags. The desire for a positive emotional connection and the allure of the perceived attributes can override critical thinking and rational evaluation. Consequently, individuals may form false correlations between the positive emotions experienced and the authenticity and trustworthiness of the catfisher. This results in misguided conclusions and values within their framework. The example of catfishing underscores how positive emotions can make us susceptible to accepting false correlations and highlights the importance of maintaining a healthy level of skepticism even in the face of seemingly positive interactions.

Cognitive dissonance arises when a person holds conflicting conclusions and values within their framework. This can happen due to early childhood experiences, social and cultural reasons, or simply cognitive biases. In any case, when people's principles are inconsistent, their reasoning may appear flawed. However, it's not necessarily that their logical processing is faulty, but rather that they maintain conflicting beliefs and realities in their mind causing cognitive dissonance and making it difficult to logically process information through System 1 Thinking. To resolve cognitive dissonance, they would need to engage in System 2 thinking and be more intentional with the shape of their framework. However, when people are already resistant to reconsideration, they may choose to live with the dissonance in their mind. This can potentially lead to mental health disorders caused by distorted realities and false correlations.

## Misunderstanding Others' Intentions

It is also common for individuals to feel misunderstood by others, despite their efforts to communicate clearly. Charles Cooley's theory of "the looking glass self" [58] proposed that our sense of self develops through our interactions with others. We imagine how we appear to them, and based on their reactions, we form ideas about ourselves. Essentially, we see ourselves through the eyes of others. However, the key point is that their perception may not always align with our own inner subjectivity. It's like looking in a mirror that can sometimes distort our reflection. This miscommunication can lead to frustration and a lack of understanding between people. Take the following illustration of a conversation between two medical students in a healthcare policy course. Both have ideologies driving good intentions, but it is easy to misinterpret each other's motives:

*Conservative:* Our healthcare system needs a focus on individual responsibility and market-based solutions to promote competition and efficiency.

*Liberal:* Individual responsibility? Are you ignoring the needs of the less fortunate? We should prioritize universal healthcare for all.

*Conservative:* No, you're not listening. I want to empower individuals and promote personal accountability in healthcare decisions.

*Liberal:* Personal accountability leads to inequality and limited options for marginalized communities. We need equal access and a system that guarantees healthcare as a basic right.

*Conservative:* You just don't understand. Heavy government involvement can lead to inefficiencies and fewer choices for individuals.

*Liberal:* You're ignoring the struggles of those who can't afford basic medical services. We need comprehensive policies to ensure equal access.

**Conservative:** I can't believe you're so blind. Free-market principles can drive innovation and better outcomes for everyone.

**Liberal:** And I can't believe you're so heartless. A unified system would alleviate financial burdens and create a healthier society.

The simulated conversation between the conservative and liberal students quickly turns heated as they misunderstand each other's intentions. Their disagreements intensify with emotions running high and frustrations mounting. They become more accusatory, venting their anger at one another's character as they clash over their differing perspectives on healthcare. The misinterpretations exacerbate their anger and prevents them from finding common ground or offering helpful advice.

Remember, everyone sees the world through their own lens, shaped by their experiences, beliefs, and emotions–their framework, in short. Misinterpretations can happen even when we try our best to express ourselves clearly. You have control over how you express yourself, but you cannot truly control how others interpret or understand you. Similarly, you have control over how you interpret the intentions of others, but you cannot truly know if your interpretations of them are accurate.

In the conversation between the conservative and the liberal, their escalating defensiveness can also be understood through the lens of our survival instinct. Defensiveness arises from the innate need to protect our understanding of reality as it forms the basis of our beliefs and values. Honest disagreements often stem from conflicting values, and when those values clash, our instinctual response is to defend our own viewpoint. This defensiveness is rooted in the fear that if we entertain new perspectives, we may no longer comprehend the world around us. The prospect of shifting our mental models and embracing alternative viewpoints can feel threatening as it may temporarily disrupt our sense of stability and competence. This fear of being operationally disadvantaged during the learning phase can lead to heightened emotions and a reluctance to truly listen and understand the other person's perspective. Recognizing this survival instinct and being aware of its influence can help create a more open and constructive dialogue and fostering a greater likelihood of mutual understanding and meaningful resolution.

In today's polarized political landscape, integrating others' views into our own can sometimes challenge our belonging to a specific ideological camp. As we develop more nuanced perspectives and acknowledge the value and insights from the other side, we risk diverging from the rigid boundaries set by our own camp. This integration of diverse viewpoints might lead to a loss of social standing within our ideological group as some members may perceive it as a betrayal or a dilution of shared beliefs. The fear of being ostracized or criticized for deviating from the established norms can create significant pressure to conform and maintain a strictly aligned stance.

This pressure to fit into our ideological camp often stifles open-mindedness and inhibits genuine exploration of alternative perspectives. However, it is essential to recognize that true intellectual growth and progress often arise from embracing complexity, seeking common ground, and integrating diverse viewpoints even if it means risking temporary social disapproval. This is true not only of political ideologies, of course, but by any idea-based collective whether it is religious, familial, economic, artistic, philosophical, etc. By valuing the pursuit of truth over social standing, we can foster a healthier and more inclusive discourse that transcends ideological divisions. Though it may cost us, developing a stronger framework displays intellectual humility and courage. Ultimately it is good for society as a whole.

In a final example, referencing the concepts of System 1 (fast/automatic) versus System 2 (slow/reflective) thinking, when we misunderstand the intentions of others through System 1 thinking we can overreact. System 1 thinking evolved to protect us from threats with knee-jerk reactions. But rarely in life are we trying to escape a predator in the bushes. Nevertheless, the structure in our brain still exists and can overlap into other areas where perceived slights, even to our social standing, can trigger such a response.

In examining the interplay between impulsive reactions, false beliefs, and the resulting consequences, we can observe the potential for devastating outcomes in various life circumstances. When individuals respond impulsively in high emotional states, such as feeling threatened or provoked, their immediate reactions may override their capacity for reasoned judgment and critical thinking. This can lead to actions that have long-lasting repercussions such as encounters with the criminal justice system, or a life marked by deprivation. Within a framework characterized by false conclusions, individuals are more susceptible to misunderstanding their life circumstances since these erroneous beliefs color their perception of reality. Consequently, the amygdala, the brain's center for processing emotions, can become hijacked which can lead to heightened emotional responses that further perpetuate the cycle of misunderstanding and impulsive reactions.

It is worth noting that these dynamics are often observed in less educated and lower socioeconomic communities where limited access to education and resources can contribute to a prevalence of false conclusions and a higher likelihood of impulsive responses. Addressing these challenges requires not only providing access to education and resources but also fostering supportive environments that promotes critical thinking, emotional regulation, and the cultivation of accurate beliefs to enable individuals to make more informed and adaptive decisions. This is why repairing our frameworks is of such vital importance.

# References

[49]   https://www.verywellmind.com/what-is-a-confirmation-bias-2795024

[50]      https://www.verywellmind.com/availability-heuristic-2794824

[51]      https://www.verywellmind.com/what-is-the-anchoring-bias-2795029

[52] Peters, U. (2020). What is the function of confirmation bias?. *Erkenntnis*, 1-26.

[53] Lieder, F., Griffiths, T. L., M. Huys, Q. J., & Goodman, N. D. (2018). The anchoring bias reflects rational use of cognitive resources. *Psychonomic bulletin & review*, *25*, 322-349.

[54] Cassotti, M., Habib, M., Poirel, N., Aïte, A., Houdé, O., & Moutier, S. (2012). Positive emotional context eliminates the framing effect in decision-making. *Emotion*, *12*(5), 926.

[55] Nicolau, J. L., Mellinas, J. P., & Martín-Fuentes, E. (2020). The halo effect: A longitudinal approach. *Annals of Tourism Research*, *83*, 102938.

[56] Nisbett, R. E., & Wilson, T. D. (1977). Telling more than we can know: Verbal reports on mental processes. *Psychological review*, *84*(3), 231.

[57] https://www.verywellmind.com/what-is-the-halo-effect-2795906

SEVEN

---

# *Mindfulness Towards our Framework*

The Framework Model provides a powerful tool for understanding how our conclusions and values are shaped by our experiences and interactions with the world. However, simply understanding Framework Theory is not enough to create lasting change in our conclusions and values. We must also learn to practice mindfulness and reflection to develop a deeper awareness of our thoughts and feelings and to challenge any false beliefs that may be holding us back.

## The Benefits of Mindfulness and Reflection

Mindfulness and reflection are powerful practices that can lead to greater self-awareness, mental clarity, and emotional regulation. Mindfulness involves maintaining a moment-by-moment awareness of our thoughts, feelings, body sensations, and the surrounding environment while reflection is the process of consciously examining and evaluating our thoughts, emotions, beliefs, and actions.

Mindfulness and reflection offer valuable benefits, but it is essential to be mindful of the potential risks of hyper-vigilance and mental fatigue. Constantly analyzing our thoughts, emotions, and surroundings requires significant mental energy. If we become overly consumed by this process, it can lead to mental fatigue, impairing our ability to think clearly, and make sound judgments. Striking a balance between being present and engaging in reflection is crucial. Practicing self-compassion and incorporating mindfulness and reflection into our lives in a sustainable manner is key to harnessing their benefits effectively.

Framework Theory posits that our mental model of the world is built upon correlations and conclusions derived from our experiences and interactions. Mindfulness and reflection directly relate to this theory as they allow us to gain a deeper understanding of the inner workings of our framework. By becoming more aware of our thoughts and emotions, we can better identify the correlations and conclusions that shape our values.

Practicing mindfulness and reflection can enhance our awareness of existing correlations and conclusions within our framework. By regularly engaging in these practices, we can develop a more acute sense of the patterns and connections that drive our thoughts, emotions, and behaviors. This heightened self-awareness can help us recognize when certain conclusions or values may no longer serve us or when they may be based on outdated or inaccurate information.

Moreover, mindfulness and reflection can facilitate the process of updating our framework by identifying and questioning outdated or inaccurate beliefs. As we become more conscious of our thought patterns, we can more effectively evaluate the validity of our conclusions and values. By challenging and assessing these beliefs, we can update our framework to better align with new information, experiences, and perspectives, ultimately leading to personal growth and development.

# Techniques for Practicing Mindfulness and Reflection

Practicing mindfulness and reflection involves a variety of techniques that can help us gain insight into our framework and facilitate personal growth. In this section, we will discuss some common mindfulness and reflection techniques and their impact on evaluating and updating our framework. Links have been provided to reputable sources that can give helpful suggestions on how to engage with these practices more deeply.

## Mindfulness Techniques

1. **Meditation:**[59], [60] Meditation is a practice that involves focusing our attention on a specific object, thought, or activity, such as our breath, a mantra, or a mental image. By doing so, we can train our minds to become more present and aware of our thoughts, emotions, and sensations. Regular meditation practice

can help us recognize the correlations and conclusions within our framework and enhance our ability to manage stress and emotional challenges.

2. **Body Scan:**[61], [62] The body scan is a mindfulness exercise that involves mentally scanning your body from head to toe, paying attention to any sensations or tension we may be experiencing. This practice can increase our awareness of bodily sensations and emotions, and can help us identify any connections between our physical experiences and the conclusions or values within our framework.

3. **Mindful Breathing:**[63], [64] Mindful breathing is the practice of focusing our attention on our breath, observing each inhalation and exhalation without judgment or distraction. This technique can help us develop greater awareness of our thoughts and emotions and improve our ability to stay present in the moment. As we become more mindful of our breath, we can gain insights into the correlations and conclusions that shape our framework. I learned to pay attention to my breathing in the Army. Controlled breathing exercises when running and shooting helped me perform better and remain calm in stressful situations.

## Reflection Techniques

1. **Journaling:** [65], [66] Journaling involves writing down our thoughts, emotions, experiences, and observations on a regular basis. This practice can help us gain a deeper understanding of our conclusions and values, as well as the patterns and connections within our

framework. By reflecting on our experiences through journaling, we can identify areas where our beliefs may be outdated or inaccurate and make necessary updates to our framework. My personal experience journaling helped me to understand the way it forced me to explore and articulate my emotions, which in turn helps bring clarity to the conclusions driving those emotions.

2. **Self-Questioning:** [67], [68] Self-questioning, often called *metacognition[69]*, is thinking about our thinking; the practice of regularly examining and evaluating our conclusions, values, and actions through introspection and critical inquiry. The skill of self-questioning is often promoted in education to evaluate what one is learning. This is directly applicable to our framework, because it is the network of all the things we have learned consciously or subconsciously throughout life. By asking ourselves questions like "Why do I believe this?", "Is this belief accurate or helpful?", and "What evidence do I have to support this belief?", we can gain insights into our framework and identify areas for growth and improvement.

3. **Contemplative Walking:** [70], [71] Taking a contemplative walk involves engaging in mindful walking while reflecting on our thoughts, emotions, and experiences. This practice is used in many religious traditions and combines the benefits of mindfulness and reflection helping us to gain deeper insights into our framework to better understand the connections between our conclusions, values, and actions. If walking is not the ideal activity for you, you could also do

contemplative drives or take long showers, or do any activity that is semi-active and soothing while also leaving a fair amount of brain processing energy for contemplation.

By incorporating these mindfulness and reflection techniques into our daily lives, we can enhance our self-awareness and more effectively evaluate and update our framework. This process of ongoing introspection and self-improvement can lead to a greater understanding of ourselves and the world around us, ultimately, fostering personal growth and well-being.

## Mindfulness and Reflection on our Conclusions and Values

Mindfulness and reflection are powerful tools for personal growth and self-improvement because they promote self-awareness and introspection. By incorporating these practices into our daily lives, we can more effectively examine our conclusions and values within the context of our framework and foster its growth and adaptation. The three interconnected goals of these practices are:

1. **Promoting Self-Awareness and Introspection:** Mindfulness and reflection help us develop a deeper understanding of ourselves and our experiences, enabling us to recognize patterns, connections, and inconsistencies within our framework. By becoming more self-aware and introspective, we are better equipped to evaluate our conclusions and values and identify areas where we may need to make adjustments.

2. **Identifying and Challenging Conclusions and Values:** Through mindfulness and reflection, we can bring to light the underlying conclusions and values that shape our thoughts, emotions, and actions. By examining these beliefs, we can identify any that may be outdated, inaccurate, or unhelpful, and challenge them in the context of our framework. This process allows us to reevaluate our conclusions and correlations, leading to a more accurate and adaptive mental model.

3. **Encouraging Growth and Adaptation:** Regular mindfulness and reflective practices foster a mindset of continuous growth and learning, encouraging us to remain open to new experiences and information. This openness allows our framework to evolve and adapt as we consistently reassess our conclusions and values in light of new experiences and knowledge. As a result, we become more resilient and adaptive individuals better able to navigate the complexities of our ever-changing world.

In summary, the practice of mindfulness and reflection has a profound impact on our conclusions and values as well as our overall understanding of ourselves and the world around us. By cultivating self-awareness, introspection, and a growth mindset, we can actively engage with our framework, shift our understanding of the world from the subconscious to the conscious through consideration, and ensure that it remains accurate, adaptive, and effective in guiding our thoughts, emotions, and actions.

Challenging our beliefs is crucial for personal growth and the development of a resilient framework. Remember, in Framework Theory, correlations between information cluster into conclusions, which cluster into values, which guide our actions. Mindfulness helps us recognize many of our unconscious correlations. These correlations serve as the building blocks for our conclusions and, ultimately, our values. By examining and analyzing various correlations, we allow ourselves to gain a deeper understanding of the information and experiences that shape our beliefs. This process helps us identify the nuances and complexities of our world which in turn strengthens our conclusions and values.

As we actively challenge our beliefs and consider multiple correlations, we are better equipped to form strong conclusions. These conclusions, based on a thorough examination of evidence and perspectives, contribute to the formation of sound values. Sound values are important because they serve as the foundation for our decision-making and behavior. By developing a strong, well-reasoned framework, we become more capable of making informed choices and navigating the complexities of life. This process of challenging our beliefs, seeking multiple correlations, and forming strong conclusions ultimately results in a more robust and resilient framework that can guide us through our daily lives. This is necessary because many of our correlations, conclusions, and values were formed from negative sources when we did not have the time or ability (especially if they formed while we were young) to critically evaluate them.

# Critical Thinking, Skepticism, and Due Diligence

Our framework is constantly influenced by external factors, including the people, environments, and situations we encounter. While some of these influences may be positive, others can be harmful and lead to negative consequences within our framework. Negative influences can introduce false correlations, biases, or misinformation which can distort our conclusions and compromise our values. For example, in 1987 the Federal Communications Commission (FCC) abolished the "Fairness Doctrine" requiring broadcast media to present multiple viewpoints on issues of public interest.[72] This has been considered a major turning point in the polarization of our news outlets which regularly use forms of bias in reporting.[73] Many of us solely consume news sources that reinforce our pre-established beliefs, rather than offering new ideas or perspectives, which is a great example of the confirmation bias discussed before. Now more than ever we need to be intentional about seeking out the sources and perspectives of our information. It is essential to be aware of the power of external influences and to recognize their potential impact on our beliefs and decision-making processes.

To protect our framework from the damage caused by negative influences, we must first learn to recognize them. This involves developing a heightened sense of self-awareness and critical thinking skills, which can help us identify instances where our conclusions and values may be compromised by external factors. Once we have recognized these harmful influences, we can take steps to mitigate their impact on our framework. This may involve seeking alternative perspectives, engaging in critical self-reflection, or distancing ourselves from sources of negative influence. By proactively recognizing and addressing harmful influences, we can maintain the integrity of our framework and ensure that our conclusions and values remain grounded in accurate, reliable information.

The ability to think critically, apply skepticism, and practice due diligence is essential for maintaining a healthy and accurate framework. These skills enable us to examine our conclusions and values in an objective and rational manner. Here are the key components of critical thinking, skepticism, and due diligence:

1. **Cultivating critical thinking and skepticism:** Developing the ability to analyze information, assess its validity, and draw reasoned conclusions is crucial for strengthening our framework.[74] Skepticism allows us to question the information we receive and encourages us to seek evidence before accepting claims. By objectively examining evidence and thoughtfully considering its implications, we can minimize the risk of forming false correlations and experiencing cognitive dissonance. This approach allows us to maintain a coherent and accurate framework that aligns with reality.

2. **Embracing open-mindedness and questioning assumptions:** Being open to alternative viewpoints and willing to challenge our own assumptions helps us to avoid dogmatism and promotes a more accurate understanding of the world.[75] This openness fosters a flexible and adaptable framework that can incorporate new information and perspectives.

3. **Evaluating sources and seeking diverse perspectives:**
Assessing the credibility of information sources and
actively seeking out diverse perspectives contribute to a
more comprehensive understanding of the world.[76] By
considering multiple viewpoints, we can identify
potential biases, blind spots, and limitations in our own
thinking and strengthen our framework accordingly.

By applying critical thinking, skepticism, and due diligence to
our thought processes, we can refine our framework and
better navigate the complexities of our world. This not only
enhances our understanding but also empowers us to make
more informed decisions and develop a more accurate
worldview.

# References

[58]       https://www.simplypsychology.org/charles-cooleys-
looking-glass-self.html

[59]       https://www.nccih.nih.gov/health/meditation-and-
mindfulness-what-you-need-to-know

[60]                https://www.mayoclinic.org/tests-
procedures/meditation/in-depth/meditation/art-20045858

[61] https://www.healthline.com/health/body-scan-meditation

[62] https://ggia.berkeley.edu/practice/body_scan_meditation

[63] https://ggia.berkeley.edu/practice/mindful_breathing

[64]         https://www.mayo.edu/research/labs/mindful-breathing/videos

[65]
https://greatergood.berkeley.edu/article/item/
how_journaling_can_help_

[66]
https://www.urmc.rochester.edu/encyclopedia/content.aspx?
ContentID=4552&ContentTypeID=1

[67]    https://www.mentalhelp.net/blogs/the-benefits-of-self-questioning-part-one/

[68]         https://blog.innerdrive.co.uk/the-power-of-self-questioning

[69] https://cft.vanderbilt.edu/guides-sub-pages/metacognition/

[70]
https://www.spiritualityandpractice.com/practices/practices/
view/27910/walks

[71]        https://www.spiritualityhealth.com/a-contemplative-walking-practice

[72]        https://en.wikipedia.org/wiki/FCC_fairness_doctrine

[73] University of Michigan.: News bias explored—The art of reading the news (2014). http://umich.edu/~newsbias/. Accessed 01 Aug 2018

[74] Lai, E. R. (2011). Critical thinking: A literature review. *Pearson's Research Reports*, 6(1), 40-41.

[75] Baehr, J. (2011). The structure of open-mindedness. *Canadian Journal of Philosophy*, 41(2), 191-213.

[76] Chen, S., Khashabi, D., Yin, W., Callison-Burch, C., & Roth, D. (2019). Seeing things from a different angle: Discovering diverse perspectives about claims. *arXiv preprint arXiv:1906.03538*.

EIGHT

---

# *Questioning Our Framework*

I n this chapter we delve into the transformative power of questions. We explore the profound impact that effective questioning can have on understanding our own framework and that of others. As discussed in Chapter 1, entering a stage of *consideration* is crucial as we examine our beliefs and values. Here, we dive deeper into the intricate workings of this process guided by the theory that questions are the primary mechanism for altering our frameworks. Whether posed by a third party or through our internal dialogue, questions hold the key to unlocking new perspectives and catalyzing personal growth. Throughout this chapter, we will uncover strategies for asking incisive questions that propel us on a path of profound self-discovery and meaningful dialogue with others.

# The Power of a Question: Socratic Method, Science, & Students

Questions play a crucial role in exploring the framework as they can help us identify underlying beliefs and assumptions that shape our thinking. By asking targeted questions, we can uncover biases, contradictions, and gaps in our understanding. Engaging in questioning allows us to explore our conclusions and values more deeply, ultimately leading to a more accurate understanding of ourselves and the world around us. This is well exemplified in the Socratic method or Socratic questioning.[77]

The Socratic method is named after the ancient Greek philosopher Socrates (469/470 BCE - 399 BCE). Socrates was known for his practice of questioning and challenging the beliefs of his fellow Athenians in public spaces such as the agora. His approach was based on the belief that knowledge could be discovered through questioning and critical thinking rather than relying on dogma or tradition. Socrates did not leave any written records of his teachings, and much of what we know about his method comes from the writings of his students such as Plato and Xenophon. Today, the Socratic method is still used in various fields, including education, law, and philosophy, as a way of promoting critical thinking and stimulating productive discussions.

The Socratic method is a form of questioning that encourages individuals to critically examine their beliefs, assumptions, and ideas. It involves a dialogue between a teacher and a student. The teacher asks a series of questions designed to challenge the student's thinking and uncover any inconsistencies or gaps in their knowledge. The student is encouraged to think deeply about their responses and to consider alternative perspectives and solutions[78].

The Socratic method is useful in developing our thinking today because it promotes intellectual humility, critical thinking, and self-reflection. By questioning our own beliefs and assumptions, key principles of Framework Theory, we can become more aware of our own biases and limitations. We can develop a more nuanced and sophisticated understanding of the world around us. Additionally, the Socratic method can be used to facilitate productive discussions and debates as it encourages individuals to listen to and consider multiple perspectives rather than simply defending their own point of view. Ultimately, the Socratic method can help us to become more thoughtful, open-minded, and effective thinkers, both in our personal and professional lives.

Asking good questions is a fundamental component of critical thinking and problem-solving. This is well understood by those who ask questions for a living: scientists. Formulating research questions and testable hypotheses are the foundation of scientific inquiry. Additionally, asking questions can help to promote curiosity, creativity, and innovation which are key attributes of scientific discovery and exploration[79], [80].

Not only scientists, but students benefit from asking good questions. One of the key benefits of asking good questions is that it can help to facilitate deep learning and conceptual understanding. In one study, students who were encouraged to generate their questions during a math lesson outperformed those who were not on a subsequent test of conceptual understanding[81]. Similarly, another study found that students who were asked to generate questions during a reading task showed better comprehension and recall than those who were not prompted to ask questions[82]. These studies suggest that asking questions can be an effective way to promote active engagement and deeper learning which can lead to better academic performance and long-term knowledge retention.

While the power of good questions has been known in the philosophical and academic realms for a long time, Framework Theory invites you to apply this powerful skill to your own beliefs and the beliefs of others. This practice encourages us to examine the underlying assumptions, correlations, and conclusions that form our frameworks. This process fosters self-awareness and helps us to identify areas where our frameworks may need to be updated or refined.

When we question the truthfulness and accuracy of the information we encounter and the beliefs we hold, we are forced to think critically about our internal correlations, conclusions, and values. This process allows us to identify inconsistencies, gaps, and inaccuracies in our framework and take steps to address them.

Engaging in regular questioning helps us to cultivate a more resilient and adaptable framework. By identifying weaknesses and inaccuracies in our conclusions and values, we can work to strengthen our understanding and develop a more coherent and accurate worldview.

# Studies on Learning to Ask Better Questions

Several studies have explored ways to improve individuals' ability to ask complex questions and engage in more productive learning, reflection, and discussions. The studies mentioned here suggest that question-asking strategies can be developed through instruction and practice, and that metacognitive, thinking about our thinking, strategies may be particularly effective in improving question-asking skills. By developing these skills, individuals can become better communicators, critical thinkers, and problem solvers.

King and Kitchener's Reflective Judgment Model proposes stages of development in individuals' ability to engage in reflective thinking and complex problem-solving[83]. The stages are as follows:

Stage 1- Pre-reflective Thinking: In the first stage of the Reflective Judgment Model, individuals rely on absolute certainty and simple, black-and-white answers. They believe there is only one correct answer and struggle to consider alternative perspectives or uncertainties.

Stage 2- Quasi-reflective Thinking: Moving to the second stage, individuals start recognizing that not everything is certain, and some questions have more than one answer. They may acknowledge different viewpoints, but still struggle to analyze evidence or think critically about complex issues.

Stage 3- Reflective Thinking: In the final stage, individuals reach a more advanced level of thinking. They begin to see the importance of evidence and reasoning to support their beliefs. They actively seek out information, evaluate different arguments, and consider multiple perspectives. They understand that not all questions have clear-cut answers, and that uncertainty is a normal part of complex issues.

These stages are not necessarily sequential, and individuals may move back and forth between stages depending on the context and the complexity of the problem at hand. The Reflective Judgment Model emphasizes the importance of promoting reflective thinking and developing individuals' ability to engage in complex problem-solving.

Martínez and Martínez's 2016 metacognitive strategy is a framework designed to help students develop their ability to ask high-level questions[84]. The strategy involves three steps:

1. **Planning:** Before asking a question, students are encouraged to reflect on what they already know about the topic and what they hope to learn. This step helps them to focus their inquiry and avoid asking questions that are too broad or vague.

2. **Monitoring:** As students ask and answer questions, they are encouraged to reflect on their own thought processes and to identify any biases or assumptions that may be influencing their thinking. This step helps them to become more aware of their own cognitive processes and to develop more sophisticated questioning strategies.

3. **Evaluation:** After the discussion or inquiry is complete, students are encouraged to reflect on what they have learned and to evaluate their own questioning strategies. This step helps them to identify areas where they could improve their questioning skills and to set goals for future inquiry.

Overall, the metacognitive strategy developed by Martínez and Martínez aims to help students become more thoughtful and intentional questioners, capable of asking questions that are more complex and thought-provoking. The strategy emphasizes the importance of metacognition and self-reflection in developing effective questioning skills.

Wilson, O'Brien, and Parks' 2013 classroom intervention aimed at improving students' ability to ask high-level questions.[85] The intervention involved several components:

- **Explicit instruction:** Students were explicitly taught how to ask high-level questions. The instruction included examples of good and bad questions as well as strategies for formulating open-ended questions.

- **Practice:** Students were given opportunities to practice asking high-level questions in a safe and supportive environment. The practice sessions included feedback from the teacher and peers.

- **Feedback:** Students received feedback on their question-asking skills, both from the teacher and from their peers. The feedback was designed to be specific and actionable, helping students to identify areas where they could improve.

- **Reflection:** Students were encouraged to reflect on their own question-asking skills and to set goals for improvement. The reflection process helped students to become more aware of their own thinking processes and to develop more effective questioning strategies.

Overall, the classroom intervention developed by Wilson, O'Brien, and Parks aimed to help students become more skilled at asking high-level questions. The intervention emphasized the importance of explicit instruction, practice, feedback, and reflection in developing effective questioning skills. The intervention was found to be effective in improving students' ability to ask high-level questions, suggesting that such strategies can be taught and developed through targeted instruction and practice.

While each of the above examples differ, what they have in common is an understanding that we can improve our ability to ask good questions. This is crucial to Framework Theory as it is a model for understanding where our patterns of thinking came from and changing them for the better. While the science of asking good questions may continue to evolve, there are a few distilled essentials that have stood the test of time that we turn to next.

# Effective Questioning Strategies for the Framework

Some key strategies are outlined below. With each questioning strategy two examples are provided. To illustrate the breadth of topics this skill can prove helpful with, the first of each example is political and the second is about parenting:

Ask questions that are:

1. **Open-ended:** Open-ended questions allow for more detailed and nuanced responses and can help us better understand the complexity of an individual's framework. Closed questions can usually be answered with a simple yes or no and limit the depth of responses we can glean.

Examples:

- Political: Instead of "Is my political view right?" an open-ended question might sound more like, "What were some of the biggest influences on my current political view?

- Parenting: Instead of "Am I a good parent?" an open-ended question might sound more like, "What are the most recent times when my relationship with my child felt very close?"

2. **Include Follow-ups:** Follow-up questions can help us clarify and expand on previous answers and can encourage deeper reflection and self-awareness. Good questions breed additional good questions. Let what you learn build on itself.

Examples:

- Political: "Now that I have identified my biggest political influences, what other influences would I like to add to the mix?"

- Parenting: "Now that I have identified times I felt very close to my child, what might those times have had in common?"

3. . **Reflective:** Reflective questions encourage introspection and can help us identify underlying assumptions and conclusions that may be influencing our thinking. These are a little trickier to formulate, and ones we may not be able to answer immediately, but as we ruminate on them answers emerge as we have new experiences and observations.

Examples:

- Political: "Beyond talking points and rhetoric, what are the principles that matter most to me when I think about the role of government in helping society?"

- Parenting: "Beyond just feeling close, when do I feel the most pride in my child?"

4. **Hypothetical:** Hypothetical questions can help us explore alternative perspectives and challenge our existing conclusions and assumptions. These questions allow us to use our creativity in imagining situations or

experiences that might push our boundaries of current knowledge or ideas.

Examples:

- Political: "If someone I really respected had an alternate political view from me on 'X' point, what reasoning do they have that I might find somewhat compelling?"

- Parenting: "What other traits or behaviors do I see in my child that I might choose to express more overt pride in to encourage more of?"

Each of these questioning strategies are ways of reframing our thinking to open up greater possibilities for growth and a healthy framework. These are also some of the types of questions a qualified mental health counselor or skilled teacher might ask us. But if we develop the practice of asking these kinds of questions of ourselves, we can grow significantly in self-guided reflection. This is not intended as a substitute for seeking professional support when needed, but as a complementary practice. In fact, being a self-learner will allow us to get more out of those seasons of life when we recruit a professional to come alongside us.

Lastly, to apply questioning strategies effectively, it is important to approach the process with an open and curious mindset. Examples of questions that could be used to explore the framework include:

- What assumptions underlie your thinking on this topic?

- What experiences have shaped your conclusions and values?

- How do your conclusions and values impact your decision-making?

- What alternative perspectives have you considered?

- How would your thinking change if certain assumptions were challenged or removed?

- What experiences or information could cause you to reconsider your conclusions or values?

 We can use questions to explore our own framework or the framework of others, and to gain new insights and perspectives. In many cases the humble art of asking a good question of others is much better than simply telling them our perspective.[86] Dale Carnegie, author of the infamous "How to Win Friends and Influence People" is often attributed with the sage advice that it is better to be more interested in others than to try and make others find you more interesting. [87]

By using these and other questioning strategies, we can gain a deeper understanding of our own framework and the framework of others. This understanding can help us make more informed decisions, challenge our assumptions and biases, and promote growth and development.

# References

[77] https://positivepsychology.com/socratic-questioning/

[78] Lam, A. (2012). The Socratic method: Fostering critical thinking. Journal of College Teaching & Learning (TLC), 9(2), 121-128. https://doi.org/10.19030/tlc.v9i2.6797

[79] Ball, S., & Luft, J. (2010). Developing inquiry-based science materials: A guide for educators. Routledge.

[80] Johnson, D. R., Adams, M. J., Estrada, M., & Freeman, S. (2013). The power of active and diverse learning approaches: Achieving student success through equity and inclusivity. Washington, DC: Association of American Colleges and Universities.

[81] Kapur, M. (2014). Examining productive failure, productive success, unproductive failure, and unproductive success in learning. Educational Researcher, 43(7), 315-324.

[82] Schnotz, W., & Bannert, M. (2003). Construction and interference in learning from multiple representations. Learning and Instruction, 13(2), 141-156.

[83] King, P. M., & Kitchener, K. S. (1994). Developing reflective judgment: Understanding and promoting intellectual growth and critical thinking in adolescents and adults. Jossey-Bass.

[84] Martínez, M. C., & Martínez, R. C. (2016). The effect of metacognitive strategies on the development of questioning

skills in students. International Journal of Higher Education, 5(1), 150-159.

[85] Wilson, K. M., O'Brien, D. G., & Parks, W. (2013). Improving students' questioning skills through classroom intervention. Journal of Educational Psychology, 105(1), 120-131.

[86] Schein, E. H., & Schein, P. A. (2021). *Humble inquiry: The gentle art of asking instead of telling.* Berrett-Koehler Publishers.

[87]https://medium.com/@aqsaajaz06/why-being-interested-is-more-important-than-being-interesting-db4e337b1f0f

NINE

---

# Applying The Framework to Our Lives

F ramework Theory is a powerful tool for examining our conclusions and values, and for bringing clarity and purpose to our lives. By understanding the connections between our correlations, conclusions, values, and memories, we can begin to identify areas of cognitive dissonance, false beliefs, and work towards living in alignment with our values.

## The Framework and Leading Theories of Personal Development

Connecting the Framework Model with core ideas in human development and social psychology are important because Framework Theory is a helpful tool to understand how some of these more complex ideas fit together. We will discuss Jean Piaget's stages of cognitive development, Erik Erikson's stages of psychosocial development, and Pierre Bourdieu's theory of habitus and how each of these are more complex ways of explaining the process outlined in Framework Theory.

Jean Piaget proposed that children go through four distinct stages of cognitive development, each characterized by a different way of thinking.

- Sensorimotor Stage (Birth to 2 years): During this stage, infants learn about their environment by using their senses and developing motor skills. They learn about cause-and-effect relationships and object permanence.

- Preoperational Stage (2 to 7 years): During this stage, children begin to use symbols to represent objects and events, and they engage in pretend play. However, their thinking is still limited by egocentrism, and they struggle with concepts like conservation.

- Concrete Operational Stage (7 to 12 years): During this stage, children become capable of more logical thinking and can understand conservation, reversibility, and other concrete concepts. They also become more aware of the perspectives of others.

- Formal Operational Stage (12 years and up): During this final stage, individuals develop the ability to think abstractly and engage in hypothetical reasoning. They become capable of deductive reasoning, systematic problem-solving, and thinking about multiple variables simultaneously.

These are ways of categorizing the capabilities of the brain at early stages as our framework is being developed. By adolescence, our frameworks have taken much of the broad shape that they will have for the rest of our lives. In these crucial early years, we pick up many of the core correlations, conclusions, and values that we will continue to carry for years to come. For example, basic ideas of morality, our native tongue, concepts of citizenship, role identities connected to gender and race, and possibly even core religious or political ideals.

Erik Erikson's theory is similar to Piaget's in that it emphasizes stages in early childhood development, but it continues to theorize stages later in life as well. He proposed a theory of psychosocial development that includes eight stages, each characterized by a specific psychosocial crisis or conflict.

- Trust vs. Mistrust (Birth to 1 year): During this stage, infants learn to trust or mistrust their caregivers based on the quality and consistency of their care.

- Autonomy vs. Shame and Doubt (1 to 3 years): During this stage, toddlers begin to assert their independence and learn to control their bodies and environment. They can develop a sense of autonomy or feel shame and doubt if their efforts are met with criticism or punishment.

- Initiative vs. Guilt (3 to 6 years): During this stage, children become more curious and adventurous, and develop a sense of initiative. However, they can also experience guilt and anxiety if they are too impulsive or feel that their actions are wrong.

- Industry vs. Inferiority (6 to 12 years): During this stage, children become interested in mastering new skills and achieving competence. They can develop a sense of industry or feel inferior if they are not successful in their efforts.

- Identity vs. Role Confusion (12 to 18 years): During this stage, adolescents explore their identity and try to establish a sense of self. They can experience confusion and insecurity if they are unable to form a clear identity or if they are pressured to conform to others' expectations.

- Intimacy vs. Isolation (18 to 40 years): During this stage, young adults seek close relationships and intimacy with others. They can experience isolation and loneliness if they are unable to form meaningful relationships.

- Generativity vs. Stagnation (40 to 65 years): During this stage, adults focus on their contributions to society and the next generation. They can experience stagnation and a lack of purpose if they feel that they have not made a meaningful impact.

- Integrity vs. Despair (65 years and up): During this final stage, older adults reflect on their lives and accomplishments. They can experience a sense of integrity and fulfillment or despair and regret if they feel that they have not lived a meaningful life.

The values that are developed in our framework play a significant role in achieving a sense of accomplishment during the various stages of psychosocial crisis. Although there may be multiple ways to achieve the critical stage tasks such as identity, intimacy, generativity, and integrity, they all require a developed sense of self-awareness and personal values. False correlations, dark associations, mistaken conclusions or lack thereof, and conflicting values in our framework can make it incredibly challenging to accomplish these tasks. For instance, if someone believes that the world is a zero-sum game with limited resources and that everything should be hoarded, it would be difficult for them to feel generative. They may prioritize materialism, leading to consumer debt and jealousy towards those with nicer possessions. Such values would make it hard for them to act generously towards others with their time or resources, thereby making it nearly impossible to have a sense of giving back.

Pierre Bourdieu's theory of habitus is a concept that describes the ways in which individual actions and perceptions are shaped by the larger social and cultural systems in which they exist. Habitus refers to the set of dispositions, attitudes, and behaviors that individuals develop through their socialization into a particular culture or social class. These dispositions become deeply ingrained and automatic, shaping the way individuals perceive and interact with the world around them. For example, developing a taste or distaste for math and higher education. If a person is raised in a lower socio-economic environment where their parents do not value education, there is a greater chance that they will not see the value in taking difficult math classes or trying to get a college degree. They may determine that they prefer to work with their hands, like most of the people around them have done. In this kind of way, habitus helps to reproduce social hierarchies and inequalities as individuals from different social classes develop different dispositions and ways of being in the world that reflect their position in the social structure. Everything from one's tastes in food, recreation, and music to the draw they feel towards certain kinds of careers and intimate relationships comes out of these dispositions and tastes in the habitus.

Bourdieu's theory of habitus is similar to the concept of the framework, but with more emphasis on how it is formed by class-based social structures and how aggregate people end up reproducing patterns of social inequality and power. Bourdieu also argues that habitus is not simply a matter of individual choice or agency but is shaped by larger social structures and systems of power. The cultural capital (abilities, tastes, skills), social capital (network of useful relationships), and economic capital (wealth and income) that individuals possess can all shape their habitus and determine their position in society.

Framework Theory differs from this theory in the degree of ability afforded to individuals to reshape their habitus or framework to develop new tastes, dispositions, and ways of seeing and acting in the world. According to Framework Theory, through System 2 Thinking, an individual can rework their external circumstances over time through obtaining and processing new information, coming to new conclusions and ultimately improving their ability to perceive the world around them in new ways. For example, if a child is raised by a parent who repeats a phrase to them "you can't trust anyone" over the course of their childhood, the child may adopt this conclusion through the phenomenon of The Illusory Truth Effect, a form of cognitive bias. As they grow older and experience various interactions with others, they may find that they can in fact trust others and begin to seek more beneficial relationships with others built on trust. As they build deeper relationships and expand their networking opportunities, they may find that they have increased opportunities to produce greater income and obtain other benefits.

While Piaget's, Erickson's, and Bourdieu's theories all focus on human development, they approach the subject from different angles and emphasize different factors. Piaget's theory focuses on cognitive development and how children construct knowledge through their experiences with the environment. Erickson's theory, on the other hand, emphasizes psychosocial development and how individuals develop their identity and sense of self through interactions with others. Bourdieu's theory of habitus is concerned with the ways in which larger social structures shape individuals' dispositions and actions.

Despite these differences, there are also some similarities between the three theories. All three theories emphasize the importance of socialization and how individuals are shaped by their experiences with others and their environment. Additionally, they all recognize the role of culture and social structures in shaping individual development.

Another similarity between the theories is their recognition of the importance of different developmental stages or periods. Piaget and Erickson both proposed a series of stages of development, each characterized by a particular set of cognitive or psychosocial challenges. Bourdieu's theory of habitus emphasizes the ways in which socialization and cultural experiences shape individuals over time, though without concrete stages. Each of these are ways of explaining patterns in how our correlations lead to conclusions which then cluster into values that build up our framework. If you want to know how cognitive development evolves in Framework Theory, Piaget offers more detail. If you want to know how identity and sense of self evolves in Framework Theory, Erickson offers more detail. If you want to know how class differences and dispositions evolve in Framework Theory, Bourdieu offers more detail.

Many more social science theories of how we develop also exist that would be too numerous to handle in detail but see Appendix A for comments on several additional theories.

## Living in Values Alignment and Clearing Out Cognitive Dissonance

While one benefit of understanding the Framework Model is to have helpful language and a mental structure to more easily understand the social science on human development. Another benefit is to more intentionally re-shape our frameworks to live more intentional lives. One strategy is to identify our core values and then evaluate how our actions align with those values. This can involve reflecting on past experiences and considering how our values have influenced our decisions and behaviors.

Another strategy is to identify any areas of cognitive dissonance or false beliefs and then actively work to challenge and reframe those beliefs. This can involve seeking out new information, engaging in critical thinking and skepticism, and being open to growth and change.

Values are a significant driver for our behavior.[88], [89] Living in alignment with our values can bring a sense of purpose and meaning to our lives. It can also increase our sense of well-being and life satisfaction as we are more likely to be engaged in activities and relationships that are meaningful to us.

Clearing out cognitive dissonance can also have a positive impact on our mental health because it reduces the stress and anxiety that can result from holding conflicting beliefs. By challenging and reframing our beliefs, we can develop a more accurate and nuanced understanding of the world and ourselves.

Our conclusions and values can have a significant impact on our relationships and life satisfaction.[90] When our actions and decisions align with our values, we are more likely to experience positive relationships and a sense of fulfillment in our lives. On the other hand, when there is cognitive dissonance or conflict between our conclusions or values, this can lead to stress and strain in our relationships and a sense of dissatisfaction with our lives.

By applying Framework Theory to our lives, we can identify and address areas of cognitive dissonance and false beliefs, and work towards living in alignment with our values. This can lead to a greater sense of purpose and fulfillment, positive relationships, and increased life satisfaction.

## References

[88] Bardi, A., & Schwartz, S. H. (2003). Values and behavior: Strength and structure of relations. *Personality and social psychology bulletin*, 29(10), 1207-1220.

[89] Schwartz, S. H. (2012). An overview of the Schwartz theory of basic values. *Online readings in Psychology and Culture*, 2(1), 2307-0919.

[90] Oishi, S., Diener, E., Lucas, R. E., & Suh, E. M. (2009). Cross-cultural variations in predictors of life satisfaction: Perspectives from needs and values. *Culture and well-being: The collected works of Ed Diener*, 109-127.

# Conclusion

Throughout this book, we have explored the concepts of Framework Model and its impact on our conclusions, values, and mental health. We have discussed the importance of recognizing negative early experiences and false correlations as well as the role of mindfulness, critical thinking, and therapy in remodeling our frameworks. In this final chapter, we will summarize the main concepts of the book and provide strategies for applying these concepts to personal growth and development.

Our framework is a complex web of conclusions and values that shapes our perception and understanding of the world. Our early experiences with family, culture, and community lay the foundation for our frameworks, but it is important to recognize that our framework is not static and can be remodeled through intentional effort. False correlations and cognitive dissonance can lead to negative mental health outcomes, but with the right tools and strategies, we can work toward living in alignment with our values and achieving greater life satisfaction.

To apply the concepts of Framework Theory to personal growth and development, it is important to begin with self-reflection and examination of our own conclusions and values. We can use techniques such as mindfulness, critical thinking, and therapy to challenge and remodel our frameworks. It is also important to seek out supportive relationships and communities that reinforce healthy values and conclusions.

It is important to remember that personal growth and development is a lifelong journey, and we must continue to learn and grow. I offer Framework Theory as a tool and set of vocabulary for better understanding that process. By staying open to growth and change, and continuously challenging our conclusions and values, we can lead more fulfilling lives and positively impact those around us.

In conclusion, the Framework Model is a powerful concept that impacts our mental health and perception of the world. By recognizing negative early experiences, challenging false correlations and cognitive dissonance, and applying strategies for growth and development, we can live in alignment with our values and achieve greater life satisfaction. My hope is that readers will continue to explore and learn about Framework Theory and related theories and use this knowledge to positively impact their own frameworks, and by extension, their own lives and the lives of those around them.

# Appendices

## Appendix A. The Framework and Other Theories

Chapter 1 introduced the concept of System 1 and System 2 thinking and how they impact the Framework Model. We explain that System1 thinking relies on existing beliefs to evaluate true/false conclusions, while System 2 thinking involves more deliberate and conscious evaluation of information. This and many other psychological theories reinforce Framework Theory. Brief comments about several are listed here in alphabetical order:

**Attribution Theory:[91]** Attribution theory supports Framework Theory by examining how individuals make causal attributions for events and behavior. By understanding how attributional processes impact behavior and decision-making, we can gain insight into how the framework is shaped by our attributions and how it influences our conclusions and values. In turn, Framework Theory supports attribution theory by providing a broader structure for understanding how attributions interact with other cognitive and environmental factors.

**Behavioral Economics:[92]** Behavioral economics supports Framework Theory by examining how individuals make economic decisions based on cognitive biases and heuristics. By understanding how these biases impact behavior and decision-making, we can gain insight into how the framework is shaped by our economic decision-making and how it influences our conclusions and values. In turn, Framework

Theory supports behavioral economics by providing a broader structure for understanding how economic decision-making interacts with other cognitive and environmental factors.

**Cognitive Behavioral Therapy (CBT):[93]** CBT is a widely recognized and effective psychotherapeutic approach that aligns with Framework Theory. The CBT model emphasizes the relationship between thoughts, emotions, and behaviors, and how negative thoughts can lead to negative emotions and behaviors. This model aligns with Framework Theory in that it emphasizes the importance of identifying and challenging negative conclusions and values that may have been formed early in life and that are no longer serving the individual.

CBT encourages individuals to examine their beliefs and thought patterns and to identify any negative thought patterns of cognitive distortions that may be contributing to negative emotions or behaviors. This process is like the process of identifying false correlations and challenging existing beliefs within the Framework Theory.

CBT also encourages individuals to develop more accurate and balanced thought patterns and to practice new behaviors that align with their values and goals. This process is like the process of remodeling the framework to in alignment with our values. Furthermore, CBT utilizes mindfulness and relaxation techniques, which aligns with the strategies discussed in Framework Theory in order to manage intense emotions and reduce stress.

Overall, the CBT model supports Framework Theory by providing a structured and evidence-based approach to addressing negative beliefs and thought patterns that may be contributing to mental health disorders and limiting personal growth.

**Cognitive Biases:[94]** Cognitive biases support the Framework Theory by examining how individuals make decisions based on mental shortcuts and heuristics that can lead to errors in judgment. By understanding how cognitive biases impact behavior and decision-making, we can gain insight into how the framework is shaped by these biases and how it influences our beliefs and values. In turn, Framework Theory supports cognitive bias theory by providing a broader structure for understanding how these biases interact with other cognitive and environmental factors, and how they can be addressed to improve decision-making and reduce errors in judgment. Framework Theory can also help identify and correct cognitive biases by promoting critical thinking, skepticism, and mindfulness. By recognizing our own biases and challenging our assumptions, we can reduce the impact of cognitive biases on our conclusions and values and make more informed decisions. In this way, cognitive biases and Framework Theory support each other in promoting self-awareness, critical thinking, and rational decision-making.

**Cognitive Dissonance Theory:[95]** Cognitive Dissonance Theory supports Framework theory by examining how individuals experience discomfort when they hold conflicting conclusions or values. By understanding how cognitive dissonance impacts behavior and decision-making, we can gain insight into how the framework shapes our conclusions and values and how it influences our behavior. In turn, Framework Theory supports cognitive dissonance theory by providing a broader structure for understanding how cognitive dissonance interacts with other cognitive and environmental factors. In Framework Theory, long running and unexamined cognitive dissonance is the driver for many personality, identity, and mental health issues.

**Cognitive Psychology:[96]** Cognitive Psychology supports Framework theory by providing a deeper understanding of how cognitive processes such as attention, perception, memory, and reasoning, impact our behavior and decision-making. By examining how the cognitive processes influence the formation of conclusions and values, we can gain greater insight into how the framework shapes our perception of reality. In turn, Framework Theory supports cognitive psychology by providing a broader structure for understanding how cognitive processes interact with other factors, such as social and environmental context.

**Cultural Relativism:[97]** Cultural relativism supports Framework Theory by examining how conclusions and values are shaped by cultural context. By understanding how cultural norms and values impact behavior and decision-making, we can gain insight into how the framework is shaped by our cultural context and how it influences our conclusions and values. In turn, Framework Theory supports cultural relativism by providing a broader structure for understanding how cultural processes interact with other cognitive and environmental factors.

**Erickson's Stages of Psycho-Social Development:[98]** Erik Erikson's theory of stages of development posits that individuals go through eight psychosocial stages throughout their lifespan, each characterized by a unique conflict or challenge that must be resolved for healthy personality development to occur. This aligns with Framework Theory and can be helpful in considering the unique challenges we face in different stages of life, although the specific stages Erikson offers are difficult to empirically verify.

**Evolutionary Psychology:[99]** Evolutionary Psychology supports Framework Theory by examining how behavior and decision-making have evolved over time to increase reproductive success. By understanding the evolutionary origins of our cognitive processes, we can gain insight into how the framework is shaped by our evolutionary history and how it influences our conclusions and values. In turn, Framework Theory supports evolutionary psychology by providing a broader structure for understanding how evolutionary processes interact with other cognitive and environmental factors.

**Habitus:[100]** Bourdieu's theory of habitus suggests that people's behaviors and dispositions are shaped by the cultural and social conditions in which they are raised, and that individuals come to embody and reproduce those conditions through their actions, habits, and beliefs. The habitus, therefore, is a set of dispositions and embodied cultural capital that guides individual actions and choices and is reproduced through socialization and experience. Bourdieu's theory highlights the importance of recognizing the power of social structures and cultural capital in shaping individual and collective behavior. The habitus is similar to Framework Theory, although the habitus emphasizes class-conditioning and the perception of probabilities of life outcomes in the formation of our identity to a greater extent. Framework Theory also emphasizes individual's agency in changing their frameworks more than Habitus Theory offers tools to change one's habitus.

**Neuropsychology:[101]** Neuropsychology supports Framework Theory by examining how the brain and nervous system impact behavior and decision-making. By understanding the neural mechanisms underlying cognitive processes, we can gain insight into how the framework is shaped by our neural architecture and how it influences our conclusions and values. In turn, Framework Theory supports neuropsychology by providing a broader structure for understanding how neural processes interact with other cognitive and environmental factors.

**Piaget's Theory of Cognitive Development:[102]** This theory suggests that children actively construct their understanding of the world through a series of stages, each building on the previous one, and that these stages are based on the child's ability to assimilate new information and accommodate existing knowledge. This aligns with Framework Theory, though it emphasizes the cognitive primarily while the Framework Model is broader, encompassing identity and values as well. Paiget's theory also offers concrete stages of development which can be useful, though are difficult to empirically verify.

**Schema Theory:[103]** Schema theory supports Framework Theory by examining how individuals use mental frameworks to organize and interpret new information. By understanding how schemas impact behavior and decision-making, we can gain insight into how our frameworks are shaped by our existing knowledge and experiences. In turn, Framework Theory supports schema theory by providing a broader structure for understanding how schemas interact with other cognitive and environmental factors.

**Self-perception Theory:[104]** Self-perception theory supports Framework Theory by examining how individuals form and modify their beliefs and attitudes based on their behavior and external feedback. By understanding how individuals use their behavior to infer their own conclusions and values, we can gain insight into how our frameworks shape our self-perception and behavior. In turn, Framework Theory supports self-perception theory by providing a broader structure for understanding how self-perception interacts with other cognitive and environmental factors.

**Social Identity Theory:[105]** Social identity theory supports Framework Theory by examining how individuals derive their sense of self from the groups they belong to and how social context impacts the formation of conclusions and values. By understanding how social identity impacts behavior and decision-making, we can gain insight into how our frameworks are shaped by our social context and how our conclusions and values are influenced by our social identity. In turn, Framework Theory supports social identity theory by providing a broader structure for understanding how social identity interacts with cognitive and environmental factors.

**Social Learning Theory:[106]** Social learning theory supports Framework Theory by examining how individuals learn from observation and modeling, and how social context impacts the formation of conclusions and values. By understanding the social learning process, we can gain insight into how our frameworks are shaped by our social context, and how our conclusions and values are influenced by the behavior of others. In turn, Framework Theory supports social learning theory by providing a broader structure for understanding how social learning interacts with cognitive and environmental factors.

**Socratic Method:[107]** The Socratic method is a dialectical approach to questioning and dialogue used to stimulate critical thinking and promote intellectual inquiry. It involves a series of questions and answers that aim to uncover deeper truths and challenge assumptions, encouraging the participant to consider alternative perspectives and arrive at their own conclusions through a process of reasoned inquiry. Socrates used this method to examine concepts such as justice, truth, and virtue, and it continues to be used today in various educational and philosophical contexts to foster analytical thinking and enhance problem-solving skills. This is a helpful way of thinking about the consideration phase of Framework Theory, where we can be more intentional about the conclusions we have come to by entering a process of deep questioning of our own beliefs and those of others.

**System 1 and System 2 Thinking:[108]** System 1 and System 2 thinking support Framework theory by examining how individuals use different cognitive processes to make decisions and form beliefs. By understanding the different modes of thinking, we can gain insight into how our frameworks shape our perception of reality and how it influences our decision-making. In turn, Framework Theory supports System 1 and System 2 thinking by providing a broader structure for understanding how these cognitive processes interact with other cognitive and environmental factors.

# References

[91]      https://www.verywellmind.com/attribution-social-psychology-2795898

[92]  https://www.psychologytoday.com/us/basics/behavioral-economics

[93]      https://www.verywellmind.com/what-is-cognitive-behavior-therapy-2795747

[94]      https://www.verywellmind.com/what-is-a-cognitive-bias-2794963

[95]      https://www.verywellmind.com/what-is-cognitive-dissonance-2795012

[96]     https://www.verywellmind.com/cognitive-psychology-4157181

[97]       https://www.thoughtco.com/cultural-relativism-definition-3026122

[98] verywellmind.com/erik-eriksons-stages-of-psychosocial-development-2795740

[99]  https://www.verywellmind.com/evolutionary-psychology-2671587

[100] https://en.wikipedia.org/wiki/Habitus_(sociology)

[101] https://en.wikipedia.org/wiki/Neuropsychology

[102]        https://www.verywellmind.com/piagets-stages-of-cognitive-development-2795457

[103]        https://www.verywellmind.com/what-is-a-schema-2795873

[104] https://practicalpie.com/self-perception-theory/

[105] https://simplypsychology.org/social-identity-theory.html

[106]   https://www.verywellmind.com/social-learning-theory-2795074

[107] https://en.wikipedia.org/wiki/Socratic_method

[108]https://thedecisionlab.com/reference-guide/philosophy/system-1-and-system-2-thinking

# *Biographical note*

C harles R.W. Sears is an American philosopher and businessman who explores the intersection of human psychology, identity formation, and practical wisdom. His work bridges academic theory with real-world application, shaped by diverse experiences across military service, law enforcement, and entrepreneurship.

Charles served 11 years in the U.S. Army National Guard, rising to the rank of Sergeant, and spent five years as a Deputy Sheriff. These roles provided firsthand insight into human behavior under pressure, crisis decision-making, and the psychology of belief systems—experiences that deeply inform his theoretical work on identity and consciousness.

As an entrepreneur since age 20, Charles has founded, acquired, and sold multiple businesses spanning service industries to technology consulting. He has mentored over 100 business owners and currently serves as Chief Marketing Officer in the technology sector, specializing in AI-driven solutions for business productivity.

His books include The Architecture of Awareness: Decoding Consciousness, which has been reviewed by experts across neuroscience, psychology, sociology, and philosophy worldwide, and The Cognitive Framework Model, which presents a practical system for understanding how identity forms through beliefs, values, and behaviors. His framework is now being applied in clinical practice by mental health professionals.

A Christian, husband, and father of two, Charles is driven by a commitment to helping others understand themselves better and live more intentional lives. His work makes complex psychological and philosophical concepts accessible to readers seeking personal growth, emphasizing the power of examining one's beliefs and the possibility of positive change through deliberate self-reflection.

www.ingramcontent.com/pod-product-compliance
Lightning Source LLC
Chambersburg PA
CBHW022114280326
41933CB00007B/386